Get Me Off The Dole!

The Essential Tool-kit For The UK Job Hunter

Visit our website at:

www.GetMeOffTheDole.com

At the Get Me Off The Dole website, you can short-cut many of your on-line searches for jobs. The site has a job search engine which extracts information from many of the UK's leading job sites and is constantly updated.

Also, at the site, you'll find regularly updated links to the latest news articles, gleaned from three of the major global news search engines.

If you want to contact the author you can easily do so through the website's Contact page.

We mustn't forget about the free stuff. You can also download a number of free things to help you with your job hunting. Some of the stuff is only available to readers of this book, such as job logs, CV and cover letter templates. If you want to keep up to date and find out about the latest books, tools and tips on career development and job hunting, then subscribe to the Get Me Off The Dole Newsletter. Details are on the website.

Visit our Twitter page at:

Twitter.Com/GetMeOffTheDole

Get more info about the UK companies that are recruiting right now and keep up to date on other job related news by visiting our Twitter page! You could also get the latest UK Job 'Tweets' sent to your mobile phone by registering with Twitter and following us.

Look forward to seeing you there!

Contents

PART III - Appendices

List of figures

List of tips

List of warnings

The author has taken every reasonable precaution to ensure the information contained in this book is accurate and up to date. Continual improvements in opportunities, for job hunters, makes it inevitable that certain references in the book may be superseded eventually. The nature of the world's economy is ever changing and this will undoubtedly result in even more opportunities becoming available as time goes by.

While all attempts have been made to verify the accuracy of information provided, the author and the publisher assume no liability for errors, omissions, or contrary interpretation of the subject matter herein. Any perceived sleights of specific persons, people, or organisations are purely unintentional. Furthermore, the author is not responsible for any changes to third party websites (referenced in this book) made after publication.

In practical advice books, like anything else in life, there are no guarantees of income. You are advised to use your own judgement about your individual circumstances and act accordingly.

This book is not intended as a source of legal, business, accounting or financial advice. You should seek the services of competent professionals in legal, business and accounting/finance fields where needed.

Preface

The very fact that you purchased or borrowed this book means you're either:

- unemployed
- looking for your first job
- dissatisfied with your current job
- worried about your job security

Whatever your situation, I would like to welcome and give you as much help as possible with your job hunt. I use the term **'Job Hunt'** quite deliberately throughout this book because it is far more proactive than mere **'Job Search'**. You're now going to become a proactive job hunter with the intention of getting back into work within the shortest time possible.

No doubt you've been hearing about all of the doom and gloom the recession is bringing us today. Because of the recession you will have witnessed a number of the big companies, that have been with us for many generations, have closed their doors for the last time. These companies have made thousands, of people jobless at very short notice. There's so much competition for work lately that it can feel hard to visualise even getting a low paid job - just to cover your living costs.

The Government is coming under increasing pressure. As unemployment rises more money is being paid out from the dwindling Treasury funds to cover social and welfare benefits. The Banking industry has also received hefty influxes of cash to keep *them* running thanks to the tax payer! This means there are fewer Government-backed opportunities to help the jobless. To balance their books the Government are making it more difficult for the unemployed to claim their entitlement to benefits too. With that said . . .

LET'S PUT ALL THIS DOOM AND GLOOM BEHIND US!

. . . and distance ourselves from all of the negativity around us and get stuck into the task of successful job hunting.

> "Be vigilant; guard your mind against negative thoughts."
> *Buddha (568-488 BC)*

Remember, you have a talent - everyone has talent. We all take them for granted and assume everyone else shares the same skills too. Nothing could be further from the truth! No two people are the same. This is great news because you have unique experiences and skills to offer a potential employer that not many others possess. In the section on Self-awareness *(page 8)* we will discover that in more detail.

I'm going to be a little blunt with you now. Perhaps your main problem is that you're not aware of what skills you have to offer an employer. Because of this you're in danger of settling for less than what you deserve. This is precisely why I wrote this book in the first place.

I have coached hundreds of people in job hunting skills and I never cease to be amazed at the way many of them sell themselves short and settle for much less than their true value. However, there are reasons why people do this in the UK. We're brought up to believe that 'blowing our own trumpet' is bad manners and something to be frowned upon. In later life we end up being too modest for our own good. This 'modesty' is costing people like you thousands of pounds in lost wages.

Another reason for selling ourselves short is that we tend to 'pigeon hole' our skills and don't look beyond our own industry to see if our underused skills are valued elsewhere. We either forget or simply don't realise that many of our skills are easily transferable. We should be looking far beyond the 'cocoon' we have spun for ourselves. Losing our job feels like the end of the world. This, coupled with a fear of the unknown, can cause severe anxiety and loss of self-confidence.

Sadly, there seems to be rather fewer places to turn to for substantial help. Many job search training schemes, intended to help the jobless, fall short of giving back the confidence and self-respect that is needed by job hunters. It's just like putting a plaster over an infected wound. On the surface it looks as if things are healed but the underlying problem still remains - only to create more pain later on.

A number of training programmes are too pre-occupied with meeting Government 'targets', by getting people back into the first available job, without ever addressing their underlying concerns (i.e. boosting confidence and properly assessing skills). This is the surest way to long term failure. Many of these job hunters will soon find themselves back on the dole. Don't get me wrong, I'm all in favour of Government money being invested in any useful training schemes. However, there should be more emphasis in providing solutions to underlying employment barriers rather than succumbing to glorified league tables and target setting.

Unfortunately I am unable to reach enough job hunters to make a difference, all by myself, and this was another motivation for me to create this book for you. My sincere hope is that the contents will also be adopted by job training establishments in the UK so that more job hunters will reap the benefits. Hence the name of the book - "**Get Me Off The Dole**".

Most people, on the dole, genuinely do want to get back to work and feel patronised by their current experience. Signing on every fortnight and then justifying why you haven't yet found a job to some teenage employee of the local job centre is too much for anyone to take seriously. I for one have been in that very position more times than I would like to admit.

Throughout my training sessions I have been fortunate enough to contribute to some really dramatic changes in peoples lives. Many of whom were brought up to believe that they were 'stupid' or 'incapable' and that they wouldn't amount to much. It's no wonder why so many suffer from an acute lack of self-confidence.

Get Me Off The Dole is an extension of some of the tips and and short-cuts that I have implemented that gives job hunters like you an advantage over the so-called job seekers. This book **WILL** also have a positive impact on you!

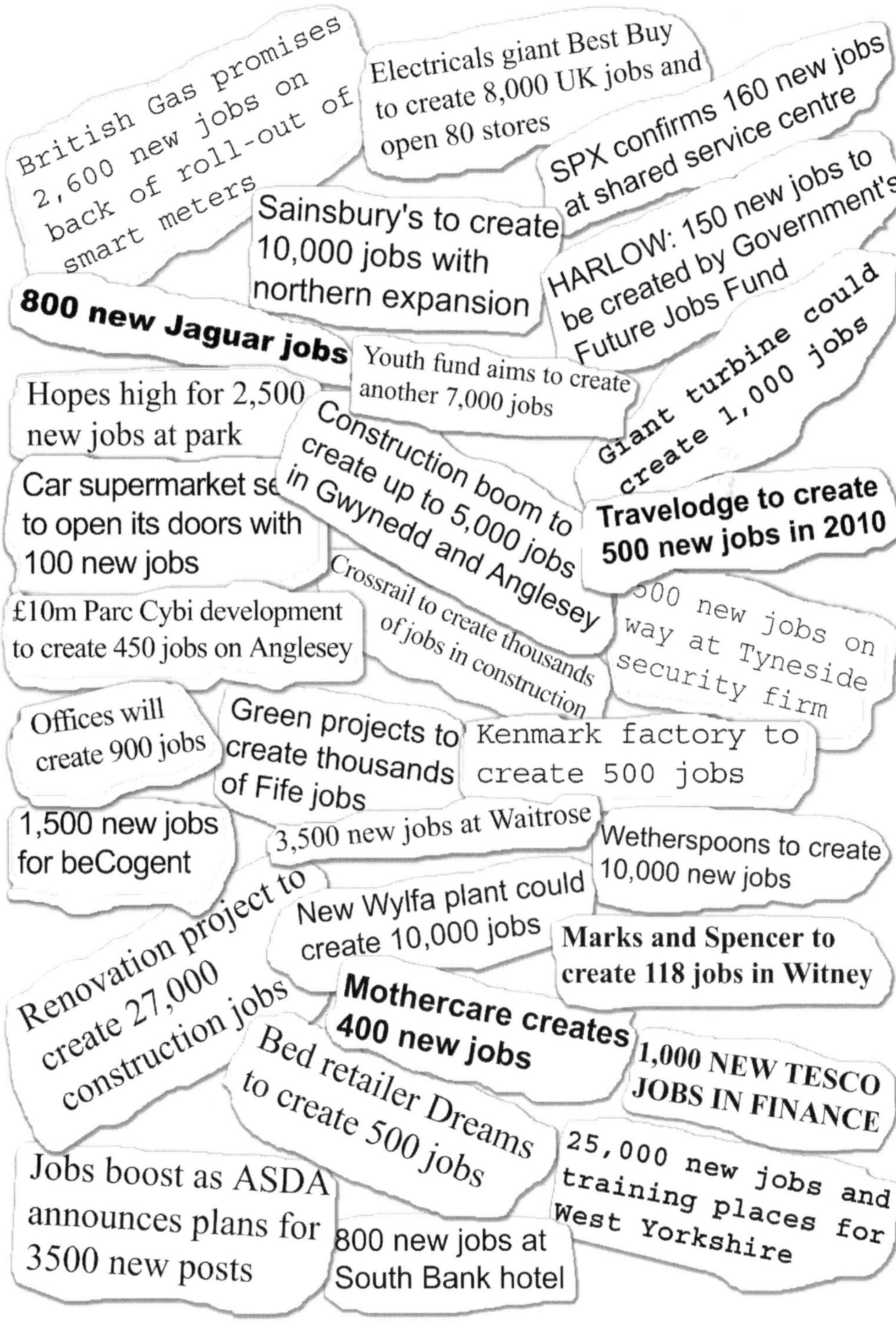

Ongoing job creation - headlines (Oct-Dec 2009)

About the author

Brian Simms is professional trainer and further education teacher who works mostly on a freelance basis nowadays. Based in Essex, United Kingdom, he teaches a number of topics including Office Administration, Computing, Job Search and Life Skills.

His students have benefited from his enthusiastic, hands-on approach. Many have suffered previous setbacks in their lives where they had lost much of their self-esteem. After only a couple of sessions with Brian, they soon realised they really do have many skills to offer an employer that they had previously took for granted. Without Brian's support they would not have re-gained their confidence quite so dramatically.

Brian is no stranger to teaching adults. Serving just over 17 years in the British Army taught him the importance of empathy and patience whilst focusing on the end results. Brian has managed to condense his job hunting strategies into this book for others to adopt so they can get back work in the shortest time-span.

As a result of many of his training sessions, it became evident that his teaching was not the norm and he has been unable to physically coach everyone who wanted tuition because of demand – hence this book.

To contact Brian, go to the **Get Me Off The Dole** website and click on the 'Contact' tab:

www.GetMeOffTheDole.Com

How to use this book

I recommend that you have a notebook and pen at the ready because there's many job hunting tips that you may have never considered before. A word of caution though; Don't try reading the book in one sitting because job hunting is quite a big task. There's an old saying:

> "The best way to eat an elephant is one bite at a time!"
> *Origin Unknown*

Therefore read the book in bite-sized chunks rather that digest it all in one go.

Throughout the book, I've highlighted several great short-cuts *(Tips)* and some avoidable pitfalls *(Beware)* with these two symbols:

Tips

Beware

Alternative URLs

You'll find many of the URLs (web addresses to people like you and me!) are rather cumbersome and almost impossible to copy out correctly into your web browser. Therefore, I have included alternative URLs to accompany the awkward ones. The alternative URLs look something like this:

tinyurl.com/sunbird-cal

When you come across these, you don't need to enter the **http://** or the **www** .

In case you're wondering, Tiny URL is an excellent resource for shortening some of the long-winded URLs. I won't give you a tutorial on how to do it here but if you go to **tinyurl.com** you can try it out for yourself.

If, for any reason, the Tinyurl link doesn't work, then replace **tinyurl** with **binurl**.

For example, instead of:

tinyurl.com/sunbird-cal

type this into your web browser:

binurl.com/sunbird-cal

Footnotes

As you read through this book you'll see that some of the items have been annotated with a number like this:

footnote[1]

If you go to the bottom of the page you will find a footnote elaborating on that particular item.

Appendices

From page 111 there are several Appendices containing valuable information and short-cuts to your job hunting success. Try to familiarise yourself with their content to that when you go through this book you'll understand how they tie in with the main content.

Taking action

By the time you have finished reading this book you will have put yourself into a better position to land yourself a great job. However, you must take action. Just reading the book will not guarantee any success.

> "Success seems to be connected with action. Successful people keep moving. They make mistakes, but they don't quit."
> *Conrad Hilton (1887-1979), Hotelier .*

1 A footnote is a reference or further explanation placed at the bottom of the page like this one.

Part I

Pre – Job Hunting Phase

Introduction

"I feel the key to job hunting is just like marketing a product. You have to really know your product before you start selling it."
Robert Jameson Gerberg (1938 -), Author[2].

First things first

As soon as you discover when your last day of employment will be, your first priority is to register with Jobcentre Plus (even if you think you'll have no problem in finding another job soon). You should give them advanced notice of your anticipated date of unemployment. This will help to ensure that no unnecessary delay occurs before getting any entitled benefits. In the first instance, you should either:

phone Jobcentre Plus on 0800 0 55 66 88 (0800 0 23 48 88 for text-phone) to make a claim for benefits

or

visit your local Jobcentre Plus. If you don't know where the nearest one is then open up your Internet browser and go here:

www.jobcentreplus.gov.uk/JCP/Aboutus/Ouroffices/Search/LocalOfficeSearch.aspx

Alternative URL: **tinyurl.com/Job-Centres**
(and enter your post code in the search box)

Once you've registered with them you'll be entitled to a range of financial benefits as well as the use of their job hunting facilities.

Don't forget to get in touch with your local council offices to see if you're eligible to pay a reduced rate of council tax whilst unemployed.

If you have any outstanding loans that you may not be able to pay (including mortgages etc.) then contact the lenders as early as possible to

2 Author of "The McKenzie Scott executive job search system: our client handbook, part I", (2003).

arrange easier payments. For example, did you know that it is possible to pay just the interest until you get your feet back on the ground? Jobcentre Plus may also be able to advise you too (you may have to be unemployed for a set length of time before being eligible though).

If your finances have got 'out of hand' and you find it difficult to cope, then make an appointment with your local Citizen's Advice Bureau. Their website is at:

www.citizensadvice.org.uk

Before you can really get down to some serious job hunting you need to overcome the negative emotions of your job loss first.

Getting over your job loss

There are a three reasons why people generally give up their time to work for others. They are:

- **Money**
- **Power**
- **Status**

Your reason for working may be one or a combination of the above. Perhaps you didn't realise it was probably more than money that kept you in your last job. Maybe you were a manager and in a position of respect; or you may have worked on a production line and enjoyed the company of your work colleagues. Whatever it was that kept you in your last job no longer exists and now you're faced with the emotions of losing that job.

This is the time where most people go through a 'bereavement phase' – you are no different. Losing a job can be like losing a friend. It affects everyone in different ways. Some feel a sense of anger and others lose their self-confidence. It really doesn't matter how many times you've lost your job in the past, the feeling of 'grief' still remains the same. This is the time when you need plenty of support from your family and friends. If your company offered you counselling, then **ACCEPT** it. The worse thing you can feel at a time like this is isolation and loneliness. Let's face it – **YOU ARE NOT ALONE!**

Once you've overcome the first stages of shock then you must sit down and start making some serious decisions. Firstly, consider a short, well-earned break. Even if it means taking a week or so off. Forget about work and just enjoy yourself. If you can't afford to go away for a short holiday then take up a hobby – even go fishing, camping or play golf. Do whatever you can to take your mind off the situation and lose some of the stress.

After you've had your break, you'll be ready to get down to your job hunt with a clear and open mind. But first let's take a good look at your current health. Just as a car can't run efficiently without regular servicing, you can't become a successful job hunter without reviewing your health and lifestyle.

Job hunters' health & lifestyle

An area which is all-too-often overlooked is the job hunter's health. One of the most frustrating things to happen is to be offered an interview and go down with a bad cold or even flu. In cases like this you are not at your best and it will be rather difficult to impress the interviewer. This can usually be avoided through a sensible diet and fitness regimen. However, it is far beyond the scope of this book to go into any detail on the subject but the following notes will serve as a starting point.

Water

The average person needs around eight glasses of water a day. Although things like tea and coffee contain water, this does not count as your daily intake. Your body needs fresh water. You can take one or two two glasses of water first thing in the morning to flush out your system before breakfast. Another one or two glasses can be taken at night whilst the remainder can be spread throughout the day. At first you'll feel like going to the toilet every five minutes or so but your body will adjust within a few days.

Immune System

Your immune system can be helped if your diet intake includes some or all of the following:

Broccoli	Dark Chocolate (in moderation)
Garlic	Ginger
Goji Berries	Grape Juice
Honey	Oily Fish (Mackerel, Salmon etc.)
Pomegranate Juice	Pumpkin Seeds
Shutake Mushrooms	Plenty of fresh air and sunshine helps too!

Exercise

You should undergo three 20-30 minute sessions of exercise (activities which causes the heart to beat faster and making you break into a sweat). This helps to improve your overall well-being and immune system even further.

Morning Regimen

If you're a well-organised sort of person who can get into a routine then you might want to try the following, each morning:

Drink 2 glasses of cool water

20 - 30 mins exercise (i.e. jogging or walking)[3]

5 mins relaxing or meditation

10 – 15 mins to read something inspirational or motivational

Eat a healthy breakfast

Many people who take up this routine find they perform far better because they feel that their mind and body have been re-energised. Give it a try and see if it works for you!

General Health Matters

If your present income dictates that you can't maintain a healthy diet (especially if you are over the age of 40), you may want to consider visiting your GP for a cholesterol and diabetes test. If your health is not at it's best then this will have a negative impact on your success as a job hunter. It is so important to stay healthy by eating properly, keeping your mind stimulated and exercising your body.

Needless to say that excessive smoking, compulsive eating and excessive consumption of alcohol is something to be avoided. Your GP may be able to advise you on any of these matters.

Advice

If you want to know more then have a look at the following topics on the NHS website:

Healthy Eating Advice

www.nidirect.gov.uk/index/young-people/health-and-relationships/keeping-healthy/advice_on_healthy_eating.htm

Alternative URL: **tinyurl.com/NI-Healthy-Eating**

---

3 Three sessions a week will make all the difference.

Fitness Advice

www.nidirect.gov.uk/index/young-people/health-and-relationships/keeping-healthy/keeping-fit.htm

Alternative URL: **tinyurl.com/Fitness-Advice**

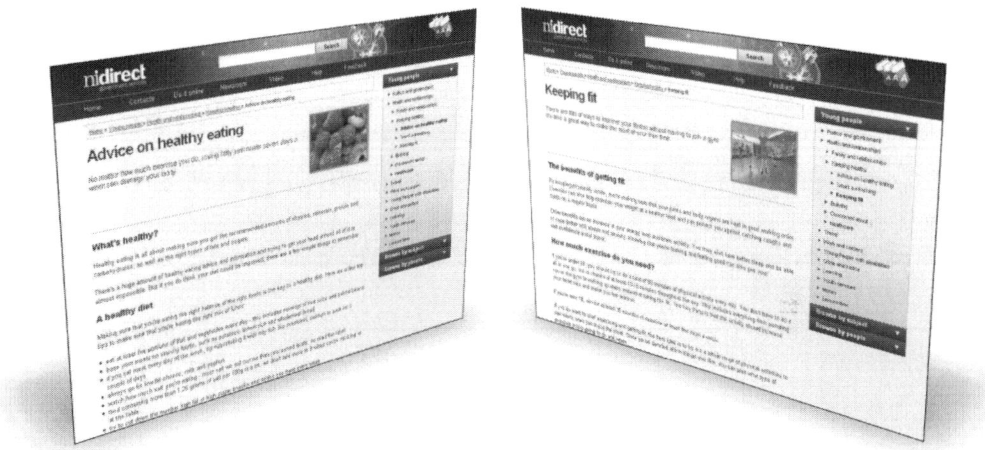

Fig 1: Government advice on healthy eating and fitness

Please note:

If you intend radically changing your diet or exercise routine, you should seek professional advice such as your GP before doing so.

Beware

Beware 1: Radical changes to diet or exercise

"It is recommended that a healthy diet should include at least five portions of a variety of fruit and vegetables (excluding potatoes) a day. In 2004, 14 per cent of men and 27 per cent of women in England consumed five or more portions a day, while 8 per cent of men and 6 per cent of women consumed no fruit or vegetables."
Office for National Statistics[4]

4 www.statistics.gov.uk/CCI/nugget.asp?ID=739

Self-awareness

> "The mind's first step to self-awareness must be through the body."
> *George A. Sheehan (1918 - 1993), Author[5] and M.D.*

Everyone is different. No two people have quite the same combination of abilities, experiences or skills. Indeed it's reasonable to assume that you're not fully aware of your own potential.

It can be quite difficult to assess your own abilities, and personality, let alone decide on what jobs you're most suited to. Whenever asked to produce a list of their abilities and skills, job hunters invariably end up with half a dozen bullet points or less.

By the time you reach the end of this section you will have amassed quite a list of abilities in which you can use to broaden your hunt for jobs. For this you will need a pen and some paper to brainstorm your inventory list.

These are what you will discover from your self-awareness profile:

- **Personal inventory**
- **Personality profile**
- **Your minimum income requirements**

Brainstorming your personal inventory

Pause for a moment until you have a pen and paper to hand and a quiet place where there are no interruptions.

Ready? Well, for this exercise, you are going to produce four lists. On four separate sheets of paper, write down the following headings (one on each sheet):

> **Hobbies** *(including sports and recreation)*
>
> **Jobs** *(including unpaid favours, voluntary work etc.)*
>
> **Courses** *(educational and vocational)*
>
> **Interests** *(anything you show an interest in, read about, but not got physically engaged in)*

---

5 Author of the book "George Sheehan on Running to Win: How to Achieve the Physical, Mental & Spiritual Victories of Running", (1992).

Hobbies

On the sheet headed "Hobbies (incl. sports and recreation)" create a summary of all the hobbies you currently indulge in, together with the ones you've done in the past (*see example below).*

Hobbies (incl. sports and recreation)

Hobby	Benefits to employer
Football	Encourages teamwork, maintains healthy body, improves co-ordination and excellent for spatial awareness.
Chess	Good at developing strategies, exercises the mind and helps to focus.

Fig 2: Personal inventory example (hobbies)

Forget about the second column (Benefits to employer) while brainstorming – we'll get back to that later *(page 13)*.

Begin by listing your hobbies as they spring to mind – don't try too hard though. For example, if you like playing computer games, write down 'playing computer games'. When you have run out of ideas, go on to list the sports you enjoy (or enjoyed in the past) even if it's just going for a walk! Afterwards, include all the other types of recreational activities you enjoy doing. It may be reading fiction, doing crosswords, meeting people etc.

Spend about half an hour or so on the list. Then take a break, go for a walk, have a cup of coffee or do something different for a short while. When you come back, have a go at the next list (i.e. Jobs).

Jobs

Perhaps you're at college, university or even secondary school and haven't had a paid job before. If that's the case you can still put together a jobs list.

This list includes all the favours and voluntary work you did for other people. It could be doing the shopping, walking the dog, washing up, cleaning, repair work, painting and decorating, going to the bank etc. Jot them all down. At this stage put everything down – even if it sounds trivial (you're not going to show this list to anyone else unless you want to!).

It may be that you had a career break, possibly a spell at bringing up a family – you can list all sorts of things here like cleaning, nursing the child, food preparation, budgeting, purchasing, banking, quality assurance (i.e. returning goods if they are faulty).

If you had paid jobs before, definitely include them too by including the job title. An example is shown below:

Jobs (incl. favours and voluntary work)

Job title	Responsibilities	Benefits to employer
Bringing up a family	Cleaning	Basic health and safety experience.
	Shopping	Budgeting, quality assurance, purchasing experience.
	Nursing children when sick	Basic first aid experience.
Favours	Cleaning	Health and hygiene experience.

Fig 3: Personal inventory example (jobs)

Tips

Always carry a notebook[6] and pen around wherever you go. You can be sure that, when you have gone for that break, one or two other items for your list will spring to mind. That's OK - just note them down and continue with your break.

Tip 1: Carry a notebook and pen everywhere

6 An A6, hard-backed, lined notebook is ideal because of it's handy size.

Don't worry about dates and employers' details at this stage. This will come later when we tackle things like CVs and application forms. Also, leave out the 'Benefits to employer' column until later *(page 13)*. All we are doing now is brainstorming your jobs list.

Courses

Since you first went to school, you've been engaged in a number of ex-curricular courses and other training sessions which kept you occupied. You might, for instance, have taken your hobbies or sports a stage further by enrolling on some course of study. If you were interested in photography, did you attend anything related, such as "an introduction to digital photography" or "art studio photography"? Were you interested in sailing and attended a "RYA basic navigation and safety" course? Do you get the idea? Now brainstorm your list of courses and training sessions (even if they were informal where no certificate or qualification was awarded).

Courses (incl. academic and and vocational)

Course	Benefits to employer
Basic computing	Computer literate and therefore won't require initial training.
First aid	Holds a valid certificate which means they could have an addition first aider too.

Fig 4: Personal inventory example (courses)

Since leaving full-time education and entering the working environment, you may well have undergone some vocational training too. Again, you don't need to have been awarded formal qualifications or even a certificate for these to be included in this list. However, if you have certificates for any of these activities, keep them handy because they will be of use when assembling your portfolio later on *(page 40)*.

Interests

This is one list that job hunters rarely put together. For this you'll brainstorm any interests that you just haven't got round to physically doing yet. For instance, you might be interested in astronomy and read a number of articles or books on the subject but don't own a telescope. You may not have joined the local astronomical society either. Perhaps you always wanted to tone your body up but have never undergone any formal training exercises or even joined a gym. You may have read some articles or books which have peaked your interest but not taken it any further.

Whatever your interest is, include it in your list!

Interests

Interest	Benefits to employer
Photography	Creative, patience with attention to minor detail. Competent in the use of digital cameras.
Orienteering	Ability to work under pressure, good navigational skills, physically fit.

Fig 5: Personal inventory example (interests)

So why should we be putting together such a list? The Hobbies, Sports and Recreation lists show things you have done in the past. Some you were passionate about and your interests may have moved on since then. For instance you might have been enthusiastic about windsurfing and now you are not so keen and you're interested in sailing instead. There may be a job opportunity related to one of your interests.

For instance, in December 2009, Lego were looking for a Master Model Builder for their new Legoland Discovery Centre in Manchester. The candidates were subjected to an unusual interview too! So even if one of your interests involved playing with Lego bricks, you could have been paid to play with them all day long! Take a look at the video:

www.youtube.com/watch?v=o1B6MBuezUA

Alternative URL: **tinyurl.com/lego-builder**

The point is that you should include all of your interests. You never know what opportunity is just around the corner.

So this list is another resource you can tap into when deciding what sort of job to look for. Just because you have always been involved in a particular job role or industry, it doesn't mean that you will easily be able to fall straight into a similar one. You might not want to. You may want to explore other possibilities and change your career path instead.

Benefits to employer

Congratulations, you have now completed the four lists. But wait. You need to go back to each item and put yourself in the employers' position. Now elaborate on each of them by jotting down the benefits to the employer. You could transfer these lists to a word processing document to make it easier to edit as you go along.

Brainstorm all the skills items on the four lists. This is going to take some time but it will be well worth the effort. If you draw a blank, go on to the next one and return later on. Ask your family and friends to join in. People like playing 'games' so treat it like one so everyone will be eager to help you.

Take a look at the examples show on the preceding pages for inspiration.

Your personality

Did you know that your own personality might be a barrier to the jobs you are applying for? One of the main reasons why people are unhappy with their jobs is because the work they do is not aligned with their own personality.

Despite what you may think, personality really does play an important part in finding the right job. For example, if you are an introvert then jobs in sales, training, performing arts etc. are unlikely to suit you. So it's vital you discover your true personality and focus on jobs to match.

A successful job hunter understands their personality traits. However, they identify their confidence levels first before getting on with the task of job hunting.

Confidence

If you've recently lost your job it is quite natural for you to have low self-esteem. It is not uncommon to feel that a failing in your abilities is what caused you to be out of a job. You may well be thinking that, if you weren't good enough in your last job, how are you going to get another? Unless you've been 'sacked' the reality is that the decision to make you redundant was a business one and nothing else. The organisation was going through tough times and had to cut their losses in order to stay in business. If the company went into receivership then it'll be quite obvious that your abilities weren't at fault anyway.

Losing your job is a depressing moment of your life and you must realise it is just that; only a 'moment' of your life. You can (and will) be able to 'pick yourself up, dust yourself down' and see this as an opportunity for greater things to come.

> "Job opportunities are like buses. You may miss a few but all of a sudden three or more usually turn up in one go!"
> *Brian P. Simms (1956 –), Life skills coach, ICT trainer and author.*

You should be aware that job hunting has its ups and downs and you'll experience a number of rejections along the way. This is normal but don't take it personally or you'll have trouble re-building your confidence again. Applying for jobs is a 'numbers game' and the more applications you send out the sooner you'll get back into work again. I'm not suggesting that you follow Thomas Edison's example though:

> "I have not failed. I've just found 10,000 ways that won't work!"
> *Thomas Alva Edison (1847 - 1931), Inventor.*

However, think of yourself as a marketer sending out direct mail. If a prospective employer is already on the lookout for what you can offer then you'll get a 'sale' (i.e. you'll be short-listed for an interview). If they are not in the market for your abilities then your application will get binned.

Direct marketers literally send out thousands of letters and are delighted when they get a 1% positive response! The only difference is that your response rate will be much higher because you will be targeting prospective employers who are looking for your skills.

There are two words which will help you win the job hunting 'game' and they are **"interest"** and **"enthusiasm"**. These two things will more than make up for any lack in self confidence that you may have right now.

Before moving on, you need to do a little soul searching to see what your confidence levels are like. Have a look at the following list and see if anything relates to you:

Do you:

- constantly find the easy way out rather than taking risks?
- usually become very nervous in the company of others, especially for the first time?
- go out of your way to avoid any form of conflict no matter how trivial?
- regularly agree with the view of others just to make them feel better despite being totally different to your own?
- get filled with dread at the prospect of being rejected?
- find any difficulty in solving your own problems?
- ever become depressed whenever things don't go according to plan and you just give up there and then?
- constantly feel the need for the approval of others before doing anything?
- frequently 'drown your sorrows' by drinking alcohol?
- get comments about any irrational behaviour?
- regularly get filled with anger with yourself (or blame others) for any lack of fulfilment in your life?
- routinely feel unworthy or uncared for?
- find difficulty in accepting praise from others who appreciate the things you have done?
- ever get accused of being a workaholic?
- feel that things always have to be perfect?
- experience a great sense personal failure if losing a job?
- have difficulty in assessing your strengths and any good points you have?

- ever drink, eat or smoke to make yourself feel better?

Be honest with yourself, how did you get on? If you agreed with any of these points then you do need a boost to your confidence to ensure successful job hunting. There are a number of ways to get help. The following suggestions will serve as a starter:

- Speak to your GP who may be able to recommend a good counsellor
- Go to the Direct Gov website for advice on "Eight ways to improve your confidence by doing":

  careersadvice.direct.gov.uk/helpandadvice/selfconfidence/bydoing.htm

  Alternative URL: **tinyurl.com/S-CONFIDENCE**

- Register for a free 6-part tutorial called "Improve Self Confidence and Low Self Esteem" at:

  www.self-confidence.co.uk

Personality tests

> "The choice of a vocation is an expression of personality."
> *John L. Holland (1919 – 2008), Psychologist.*

As I mentioned earlier, everyone is different in the experiences they've had and the lives they lead. Likewise, personalities differ between individuals. Successful companies are very much aware of this and do everything they can to employ people with similar temperaments and visions. They are looking to employ staff that match their company's ethos.

A growing number of companies rely on personality tests, as part of their application process, to filter out those candidates who don't fit their criteria for the job.

One of the greatest mistakes people make when job hunting is going after jobs which they're totally unsuited for. They may get the job but soon afterwards they realise that they are either out of their depth or the job doesn't really satisfy them.

To ensure you're on the right track, you can take a personality test yourself. As long as you're totally honest when answering the questions, you'll gain an invaluable insight into your own personality that you probably hadn't realised before.

Of course, no such test is ever going to be 100% accurate. However, if you use the results just as a guide you will see new possibilities that you never dreamt of before. It will also help you to filter out many jobs which contradict your personality.

Have a go at the personality test provided by the BBC website and see what you can discover about yourself. The test is completely free and will only take up to ten minutes of your time – there's only seven questions:

www.bbc.co.uk/science/humanbody/mind/surveys/careers

Alternative URL: **tinyurl.com/BBC-Pers-Test**

This test will get you thinking about the sort of jobs that would suit your personality and style. It is based on John L. Holland's theory of vocational choice which suggests that people with certain interests are are in favour of certain types of job. He identified the following traits in people:

Artistic
creative, original, independent, chaotic

Conventional
detail-oriented, organizing, clerical

Enterprising
competitive environments, leadership, persuading

Investigative
analytical, intellectual, scientific, explorative

Realistic
practical, physical, hands-on, tool-oriented

Social
cooperative, supporting, helping, healing/nurturing

Take the assessment and find out which is your dominant trait. You may be surprised at the results!

Knowing your personality can give you the edge over other job hunters because it can either confirm your instincts or give you a fresh insight as to the jobs that best suit you.

Another self-evaluation you might consider is a **skills and interests assessment**. Have a go at this one (however, it will take you a little longer than the personality test):

skillsandinterests.com/careersadvice

Now that you have compiled your lists and printed out your personality profile, file them away in an easily accessible folder for later use.

Beware

Please note:

The results of the assessments should only be used as guides. Any decision about your future career must not rest solely on their outcome.

Beware 2: Decisions based on assessment results

Psychometric tests

Psychometric testing is becoming more commonplace in the recruitment of employees. Despite what you may have been told – you really can't revise for these tests because every employer will have their own criteria. There's also no right or wrong answer to the questions asked in these tests.

If you have ever taken part in a psychometric test then you'll realise that some of the questions appear to be duplicated. The tests are structured in such a way that the recruiter can be alerted to inconsistencies in your responses which can lead them to believe you may be giving false answers.

It is in your own interests to answer them honestly. Failure to do so will usually have one of two consequences. Either you will fool the employer and get the job (soon finding that you're unsuitable) or you might have been a prime candidate for the job but got caught out trying to bluff your way through the test.

Even if you do not seem to do well in this test, you'll find that it is normally combined with a one-to-one interview where you can still create a good enough impression to 'win' the job.

Your minimum income requirements

Before going after a job, which appears to provide a good salary, let's find out what your survival income needs to be. Any job below this income level would be completely out of the question. Sounds obvious doesn't it? You'd be surprised at how many people get over excited about a job only to find they can't meet their daily living expenses. Make sure you're not one of them.

A quick way to do this is by using the on-line FSA calculator:

www.moneymadeclear.fsa.gov.uk/tools.aspx?
Tool=budget_calculator

Alternative URL: **tinyurl.com/Budget-Calculator**

When completing the on-line form, the part which says "Pay after tax" should be left to zero. After you have inserted details of all your income and outgoings, you will get a budget summary showing your total shortfall. This is the minimum figure you need to earn[7] to cover living costs etc.

However, this shortfall figure needs to be adjusted for each job you apply for. This is because you must allow for travel costs (to and from work) and also you need to allow for other deductions from your salary such as income tax. A quick way to discover how much tax is likely to be deducted can be found by using the I-resign on-line resource:

www.i-resign.com/uk/financialcentre/tax_calculator.asp

Alternative URL: **tinyurl.com/UK-Tax-Calc**

After you've found out what your minimum net pay is, you can discover what your minimum gross pay (i.e. the advertised salary) must be before going after after any jobs.

7 This figure does not include income tax or travel expenses.

Tips

There may be times when you want to compare job ads quickly but don't have a calculator to hand at the time. Here's a couple of quick calculations you can do in your head

– ***don't expect 100% accuracy though:***

Hourly rate to annual salary

Double the hourly rate and add three zeros. i.e. If the hourly rate is £6 then double it to £12 and add three zeros to make £12,000.

Annual salary to hourly rate

Round off the salary to the nearest thousand then remove the last three zeros and halve the result. i.e. If the annual salary is £15,750 then round it up to £16,000, remove the last three zeros to make it £16 and then halve it to make £8.

Weekly rate to annual salary

Halve the weekly rate, add two zeros and then add two weeks salary on top. i.e. If the weekly rate is £440 then halve it to £220, add two zeros to make it £22,000 and a further £880 (2 x £440) on top to make it £22,880.

Annual salary to weekly rate

Round off the salary to the nearest thousand then remove the last two zeros and then double the result. i.e. If the annual salary was £18,400 then round it down to £18,000, remove two zeros to get £180 and then double it to make £360.

Tip 2: Quick salary conversion tips

Getting organised

> "Organising is what you do before you do something, so that when you do it, it is not all mixed up."
> *A.A. Milne (1882 – 1956), Playwright and author.*

Successful job hunting requires a systematic approach and the only way to achieve this is to get yourself organised. Here's a list of essential and recommended *(page 35)* resources.

Essential resources

The following items are essential:

- **Telephone with messaging facilities (voice mail)**
- **Fax machine**
- **Computer with:**
  - **Internet access**
  - **Word processing software**
  - **Printer**
- **Email accounts**
- **Diary**
- **Job log**
- **Correspondence files**

Just in case you don't have all of these items, we'll also explore some alternatives.

Telephone

If, for whatever reason, you don't have direct access to a telephone (land line) then you really must obtain a mobile phone. If you get a 'pay as you go' account then you'll be up an running in no time. Mobile phones can be purchased for around £15 or less.

Even if you do have a telephone, a mobile phone is an extremely useful resource. Recruitment agencies and prospective employers can contact you while you are out and you don't have to be 'waiting by the phone' to receive your calls.

Beware

Mobile phone calls can become expensive so you should consider using your home phone (or public call boxes) for outgoing calls. Check with your local jobcentre to see if you could use one of their dedicated customer phones.

Beware 3: Mobile phone calls can become expensive

If you have access to a computer with an Internet connection then you can set up a free voice mail without the need of a physical land line. There are a few services that offer free voice mail such as:

YAC

web2.yac.com/jsp1/yacNo.jsp

Alternative URL: **tinyurl.com/YAC-Voicemail**

Adcall

www.adcall.com/voicemail_to_email.html

Alternative URL: **tinyurl.com/Adcall-Voicemail**

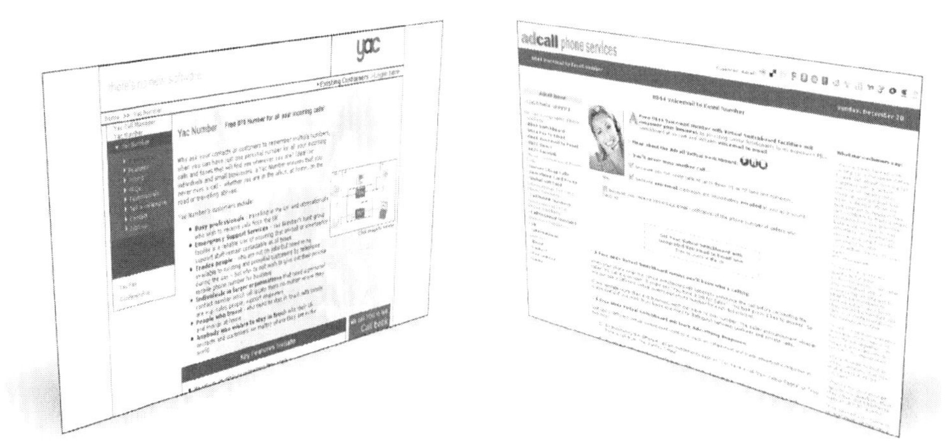

Fig 6: YAC and Adcall voice mail services

These free voice mail services offer you a contact number where messages can be sent. You'll have your own individual number which is physically located at either YAC or Adcall (depending on which service you use). When they receive your voice mail they automatically convert them to a digital sound file which is then forwarded to your email account. When you open your email, you can then play the message.

Fax machine

Having access to a fax machine is going to make life a lot easier for you. However, if you do not have immediate access to one, you could always send faxes through stationers (such as Staples) and many libraries also allow you access for a small fee. Be sure to find out if your local jobcentre can offer you the facility to send faxes. If they do, you may find that there is no charge for this so long as it is only for job hunting purposes.

If you have a computer with Internet access, you can open up a free account with on-line services like eFax. Their fax account allows you to receive faxes and you don't even need a telephone line either.

So how does it work? Well after filling in a simple form you will instantly be given a fax number. It looks very much like a mobile phone number. If someone sends a fax to this number, it will be converted into an image file and then forwarded to your email account in the same manner as the free voice mails.

To get a free account, go to:

home.efax.com/s/r/FreeUK

Computer

You need access to a computer with the following:

Internet access

Word processing software

Printer

Internet access

As a serious job hunter you must have access to a computer that is connected to the Internet. If you don't have your own, then you could either use:

- a friend's
- book a library computer (most public libraries have Internet access for their customers' use)
- use an Internet café (because it is not free you will be more focused and get more done in a shorter space of time!)

Word processing software

Most computers have word processing software installed. Although Microsoft Office contains an exceptionally good word processing application (Microsoft Word), you really don't need to go to the expense of purchasing this software. If your computer runs Windows programs then it is likely to have Wordpad installed. Just click on the start button and then select:

Programs > Accessories > Wordpad[8]

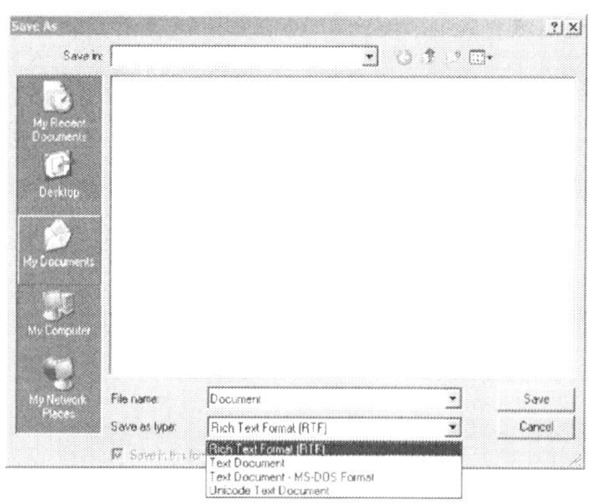

Fig 7: Wordpad dialog box

If you're using Wordpad make sure that you save your files in 'Rich Text Format (RTF)'. If you save as another file type you will lose all formatting.

RTF is one of the best formats to use if you don't have your own computer. This is because the files created can be used on any Windows-based

8 Note: This should not be confused with Notepad which has no word processing capabilities.

computer; using any word processing software and on any version of that software. Remember that, at some stage you will need to convert the files into Microsoft Word format. However, if you don't have access to Microsoft Word, there is another alternative called Writer which is available as part of a complete package from OpenOffice.org

OpenOffice.org is available to everyone for **free!** It works in a similar fashion to Microsoft Office and you can even produce files that are Microsoft Office compatible. You can download it from here:

www.openoffice.org

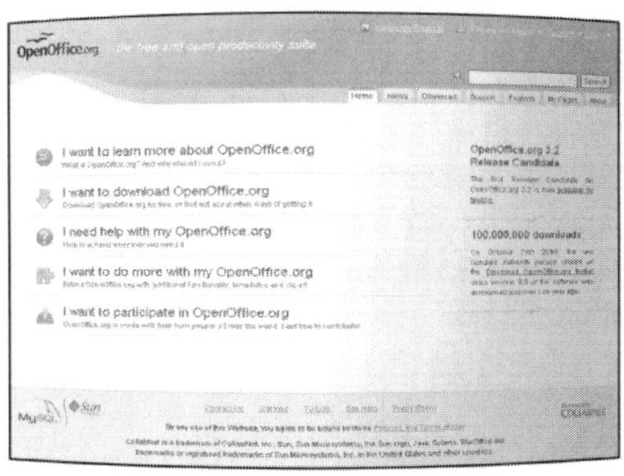

Fig 8: OpenOffice website

When you arrive at the above web page, select the "I want to download OpenOffice.org" option and follow the instructions.

Please note that, although you can save your documents in Microsoft Word format, sometimes the documents contain a slight glitch making them look a bit different. However, this is quite rare although it is something you should be aware of – particularly when putting together your CVs in Microsoft Word format.

To overcome this potential problem, download the free Microsoft Word Viewer which is available from:

> www.microsoft.com/Downloads/details.aspx?familyid=3657CE88-7CFA-457A-9AEC-F4F827F20CAC&displaylang=en
>
> *Alternative URL:* **tinyurl.com/word-viewer**

With Word Viewer, you'll be able to preview and print out your documents in exactly the same layout as anyone using the full version of

Microsoft Word. This will ensure that any lost formatting is brought to your notice before you send out documents (i.e. your job applications!).

Printer

A printer is essential. You could get away without one for most on-line job applications. However, when it comes to sending out physical letters by post and keeping hard copies of all your correspondence, you will run into difficulties without one. If you need to purchase a printer, laser printers are now more affordable than they used to be. Although inkjet printers are a lot cheaper to buy, replacement cartridges can become expensive and don't last as long as laser cartridges. You really need to shop around.

Email accounts

You must have two email accounts for successful job hunting. One is to be used for personal messages to friends, acquaintances and family. The other email account is for job hunting use only. Treat the latter as a business email account and you won't go too far wrong. I have come across all sorts of weird and wonderful email addresses which are quite humorous but would not impress potential employers. So it is essential to keep your personal email address out of your potential employer's reach.

So why can't you use just one account? There are three main reasons:

- A personal email account can be used for networking with your family, friends etc. *(page 73)*.
- Your job hunting email account needs to have a business-like appearance. After all this is one of the first things a potential employer will judge you by.
- Having separate accounts makes it easy to find messages and to respond to any job opportunities faster.

If you don't already have an email account, there are a number of good options including Yahoo Mail, Gmail or Hotmail:

MSN Hotmail

get.live.com/mail/overview

Yahoo Mail

mail.yahoo.com

Gmail

mail.google.com

These are the most popular free email services on the Internet. Each of them provides on-line access to your email so you can even view your messages whilst away from home.

Tips

Go to your **personal email** account and look for the option which allows you to use an email signature. Insert something like this:

> PS. I'm still looking for a job as an Office Manager. If you hear of any similar opening, I really would appreciate it if you'd let me know.

Using your **job hunting email** account You can make it easy for prospective employers and recruitment agencies to find your contact information through your email signature i.e.:

> John Smith
> Office Management Specialist
>
> Email: john.smith@whatever-email.com
> Tel: 0209 000 000
> Fax: 0209 000 000
> Address: 124 The Street, Anytown, Whereshire ZZ1 9AA

This saves them from referring back to your CV each time to get the info.

Tip 3: Use of email signatures

Beware

Please note:

When selecting an email address you should choose the name that the employers will know you as. For example, John Smith would be either JohnSmith, John.Smith, John_Smith, J.Smith, JSmith, J_Smith, J.A.Smith, JohnAlanSmith, John.Alan.Smith, John_Alan_Smith etc.

Your personal email account name can consist of anything. Even something humorous! Just be sure not to send off any job applications using that one!

Beware 4: Choosing an email address

To sum up, make sure you use your personal email account for your friends; and your job hunting email account for job hunting/business purposes.

Diary

Everyone has their own preferences regarding the reminders they use to keep themselves organised. Unless your memory has instant recall, then it is best to rely on a diary as a prompt.

An A4 diary with a week to a view or A5 diary with a day to a view are highly recommended for the job hunter.

Alternatively, you could print out your own pages and place them into a two ring binder. To do this, you can print off one-day-to-a-page calendars that can be downloaded from here:

blog.econsultant.com/print-2010-calendar-365-pages-daily

Alternative URL: **tinyurl.com/2010-365**

If you have Microsoft Outlook installed on your computer, you can print off blank calendar pages or, better still, use the software to do your planning and then print off the completed pages as and when needed.

Another alternative is to download a free software application called Sunbird and use that for your diary:

www.mozilla.org/projects/calendar/sunbird

Alternative URL: **tinyurl.com/sunbird-cal**

Again you can print off pages from your completed diary when required.

Whatever your preferences, you will need to consistently use a diary to keep track of your job hunting appointments and tasks.

Tips

If you're in the habit of losing your diary or there are some very important appointments coming up in the future, (such as job fairs, courses etc.) then you can also use a free on-line service such as **Freeminder**:

www.freminder.com

After you've registered with them, you can enter important dates (even birthdays!) and when that day comes along, you'll automatically get an email reminder!

Don't forget your mobile phone. Even cheap mobile phones allow you to set up a reminder. Take a look at the instruction manual and try it out!

Tip 4: Email/mobile phone reminders

Job logs

If you are keeping your diary up to date, you may be wondering why you should also keep a job log. There are two reasons for this:

- If you're registered with Jobcentre Plus, they stipulate that you must keep a job log which you should take with you each time you sign on.
- Organised job hunters keep logs with their job-related correspondence to keep track. Your diary will serve as a chronological overview of events.

Standard job log

If you are going to take your job hunting seriously then you'll soon realise that the standard job log, recommended by Jobcentre Plus *(page 30),* is insufficient for your needs. Organised job hunters will find the Progressive job log a great asset.

What I did	Date	What happened	What I will do next	When

Fig 9: Standard job log

Progressive job log

The progressive job log *(pages 30 and 121)* is an important part of a successful job hunting strategy. You may find it easier to use if you put this onto a spreadsheet. If you don't have access to Microsoft Office (Excel), then use OpenOffice.org Calc instead. If you haven't already downloaded OpenOffice.org for the word processing application, you should do so now because the software also contains the spreadsheet software too *(page 25)*:

www.openoffice.org

Incidentally, the spreadsheet produced by this application can also be saved in Microsoft Excel format too!

If you feel more comfortable using a word-processor by all means use that instead. Ensure that the page orientation is changed from portrait to landscape to fit the columns in and also choose smaller font size. A full-page example is shown on page 121.

Folio (Application No)	Organisation/Company	Contact	Source	CV Sent	1st Follow Up Call	2nd Follow Up Call	1st Interview	1st Thank You Letter	3rd Follow Up Call	2nd Interview	2nd Thank You Letter	4th Follow Up Call	Outcome	Comments
23	ABC, Welding Co Ltd	John Hammond Tel: 0203 111 222 ext 159	The Times 21/04/08	Ver. 3 22/04/08	06/05/08 Still vacant	-	13/05/08	14/05/08	-	Not short-listed	-	-	-	Over-qualified for job!
24														

Fig 10: Progressive job log

The headings are explained in detail below. In these examples (particularly in the follow up phone calls and interviews) we shall be tracking a 'fictitious' folio (application) number 23:

Folio (Application No)

Your Log should have serial numbers starting from 1. Each row refers to only one job application. If you apply for two or more jobs with the same company then you will need to have two or more rows for the same company.

Organisation/Company

Just the organisation/company name and town/city should be sufficient.

Contact

A contact name, appointment and means of getting in touch with them, should be inserted here.

Source

Just the source of the job ad and the date needs to be inserted here.

CV sent

Insert the date your covering letter and CV were sent. You will be adjusting your CV as you go along and will have a number of different versions going around. If this is the case then you need to keep track of which version you have sent by including the version number of your CV.

1st follow up call[9]

To ensure you make your 1st follow up call in plenty of time, make a note in your diary (choosing a date which is two clear working days before the closing date). You could abbreviate it like this:

1st Fol Up App 23

If you get confirmation that your application was received, then make a note of the date in the 1st follow up call box of the progressive job jog and cross out the reminder in your diary.

If you do make the call, then enter the date in the progressive job log and tick off the reminder in your diary as having been completed.

9 Follow up calls are made to ensure that the applications are managed properly and allows time to rectify anything lost in transit without missing the deadlines unnecessarily.

A suggested follow up call script for this is outlined on page 116.

2nd follow up call

To ensure you make your 2nd follow up call on time, make a note in your diary (choosing a date which is two clear working days after the closing date). You could abbreviate it like this:

2nd Fol Up App 23

If you receive an invitation (or a rejection) for an interview then put a line through the 2nd follow up call box of the progressive job log. In this case you won't need to make the 2nd follow up.

Keep the 'door' open

If your application is unsuccessful, send a final ("keep the door open") letter to the hiring manager. *A suggested format is on page 123.* This shows them you are still interested and that, if the successful candidate does not actually take up the post (believe me, it does happen) then the company won't have far to look for someone else!

If you do make the call, then put the date in the 2nd follow up call box and tick off the reminder in your diary as having been completed.

A suggested follow up call script for this is shown on page 118.

1st interview

When you receive notification of your first interviews, put the date in this box. If the interview is in another location to where your application was sent to, then also include the name of that location here.

Make a note of the interview date in your diary. You could abbreviate it like this:

1st Int App 23

As soon as you have received confirmation of your 1st interview, begin your preparations **today** – see page 93 for more details.

1st interview thank you letter

Within 24 hours of attending your 1st interview, send a thank you letter to the main interviewer/hiring manager. It doesn't matter whether you think the interview went well or not. Not only is it a matter of courtesy, but a lot of job hunters won't even consider this. The interviewer/hiring manager will remember your letter which gives you a greater chance of being short-listed further or even offered the job.

A suggested thank you letter is shown on page 122.

3rd follow up call

If the interviewer said that you will be notified of the outcome within a certain number of days, then make a note in your diary to contact them the day they promised. If you were just told that they would just be in touch then make a note in your diary (choosing a date which is three clear working days after the interview). You could abbreviate it like this:

3rd Fol Up App 23

If you hear nothing, then make the 3rd follow up call. *A suggested follow up call script for this is on page 119.*

Should your application be unsuccessful then immediately send out a "Keep the door open" letter *(page 123).* If this is the case then put a note to this effect in the 'Outcome' box of the log and the words "**CLOSED**" and "**Door opener sent**" (with the date) in the Comments box.

2nd interview

In many cases only one interview is required before the hiring manager decides who to employ. However, this is not always the case and a second interview may be required.

If you receive an invitation to a second interview, put the date in this box and make a note in your diary. You could abbreviate it like this:

2nd Int App 23

You'll need to brush up and begin your preparations **today** – see page 93 for more details.

2nd interview thank you letter

If you were not invited to a 2nd interview then this is irrelevant. However, just like the first interview, follow it up within 24 hours with another thank you letter. Ensure you enter the date in the log. A suggested 2nd thank you letter is on page 122.

4th follow up call

See second follow up call for details – page 32.

Outcome

Enter the brief details of any outcome.

Comments

Enter any notes which you think would be helpful to you. If you have applied for other jobs through the same company or used the same recruitment agency, cross-reference the other folio numbers here. If you haven't been offered the job (or accepted it) and you no longer need to do any work on it, put the word "**CLOSED**" in large capital letters in this box.

Keeping the **progressive job log** up to date is not as complicated as it sounds. You can create your own system if you want but do make sure you are consistent. Tracking your job applications is vital for success.

Correspondence files

Your correspondence files consist of two lever-arch files. One to be used for current applications and the other for closed ones.

Every communication sent to prospective employers/recruitment agencies need to be filed away for easy access. It is no good trying to save paper by keeping all your correspondence stored on the computer. Computers have a habit of letting you down when you need them the most! If your computer's hard drive crashes or a virus wipes out some of your data then you really do have a problem.

The simplest way to keep tabs on everything is to print out a copy of each job application. In the top right hand corner of the printout insert the folio number corresponding to the progressive job log *(page 30)*. For example, the job application, correspondence and any other notes relating to "ABC Welding Co Ltd" should be placed together (in date order). You may prefer to insert them in a PVC poly-pocket to keep them together.

Every time you need to refer back to your application these documents will now be easily accessible.

At the front of the folder should be a contents sheet which consists of a print out of the spreadsheet.

Tips

To save on laser toner or ink cartridges you can set your prints to draft quality. In most cases you won't even notice the difference in quality but you will see a difference in the reduction of ink/toner cartridges that you have to buy!

Instead of paying for branded toner and ink cartridges, why not buy compatible ones and save more money.

If your local stationers don't have the cartridge you want, I personally use the following on-line supplier where I've consistently received delivery within one working day:

www.justlasers-plus.co.uk

Tip 5: Economising on printer cartridges

Recommended resources

Although they are not absolutely essential, the following items are highly recommended for the job hunter:

- **Spell checking software**
- **Networking lists**
- **Business cards**

Spell checking software

No-one is infallible and spelling mistakes are common. However, this is one area where prospective employers weed out many job applications because of spelling errors. Most of which could have easily been avoided.

Off-line

Practically all word processing applications[10] have their own built-in spell-checkers and it is surprising how many people never check what version is being used (i.e. USA or UK). Having a USA version to mail letters to UK addressees is just asking for problems. For example, I've seen many letters and CVs which appear to be spelt incorrectly because the spell

10 Microsoft Wordpad is one exception.

checking software used the American-English version of the built-in dictionary!

Also with a spell checker, some words can be spelled correctly but they are out of context. Therefore you still need to manually go over your work to ensure it is right.

An example of some words which are spelled correctly but are out of context with each other are:

here, hear

right, write, rite

You should also invest in a good English dictionary and have it readily available for job hunting. They can be picked up at reasonable prices everywhere.

On-line

Most spelling errors occur when filling out on-line forms. This is because there seems to be some sort of urgency about them. If you are using Microsoft Internet Explorer, then it is recommended that you download the following spell checker:

www.iespell.com/download.php

Once the program has been activated, it sits on the tool bar of Internet Explorer and helps to avoid unwanted typos when completing on-line forms.

If you are working on-line, two excellent dictionary resources you should bookmark are:

www.askoxford.com

dictionary.cambridge.org

Networking lists

These are lists of all your contacts, acquaintances, friends and family. They can be put on a spreadsheet or listed on lined paper. To network effectively you need to put together the following contact/networking lists:

- **Family**
- **Acquaintances**
- **Friends**
- **Ex work colleagues**

A suggested example of a friends' contact list is shown below:

Friends' Contact List

Name	Means of contact	Frequency of Contact	Last contacted	Comments
Jim Smith	Tel: 0203 123 789	Fortnightly	24/05/2008	
June Adams	145 New Street, Anytown, Countyshi re AZ9 2MM	Monthly	01/04/2008	

Fig 11: Example of a friends' networking list

Your lists may be small at first but they will be added to as you recall long-lost friends and acquaintances. As you meet new people, put them on the appropriate list too. Don't just restrict yourself to the four lists shown above. Add as many others as you need.

Once you've put together your initial lists make a point of contacting each person on a regular basis. The frequency of contact will largely depend on how well you know each person. Obviously close friends would be contacted more frequently than acquaintances.

So why should we be contacting these people? In short, you will be using these lists as a means of networking with people you know. Each time you contact them, you should also be mentioning the fact that you are looking for work. Tell them how much you'd appreciate them contacting you if they hear of anything that's even close to the sort of job you're after.

Before you start sending out personal emails to them, make sure your email accounts are set up so they automatically add a signature with a PS and an extra message *(see the tips on page 27)*.

Business cards

Business cards are generally associated with people in jobs. However, they are a powerful tool for the people in your network too *(page 36)*. Give everyone in your network a handful of your business cards. If any come into contact with someone who may help you (i.e. prospective employers) they can mention you and hand over one of your cards.

A personal business card should consist of your name, your specialism (type of work you're looking for), any appropriate qualifications, home address, telephone number and email address printed on it.

You can either go to your local printers or stationers and order them or even get inexpensive ones (which you can design yourself) from Vista Print:

www.vistaprint.co.uk

Some more information and sample layouts are available from:

www.utm.utoronto.ca/careers/pdf/Networking_Business_Cards.pdf

Alternative URL: **tinyurl.com/bcard1**

www.1st-writer.com/businesscards.htm

Alternative URL: **tinyurl.com/bcard2**

Business cards do not have to be standard ones made from card. The more unusual they are the better as these are more likely to get noticed. For instance, Lego have very innovative and unusual ones for their staff. Their 'cards' are actually Lego toy figures, that resemble individual staff members, with their details printed on them. Have a look yourself:

www.guardian.co.uk/lifeandstyle/gallery/2009/mar/26/lego-pictures?picture=345081223

Alternative URL: **tinyurl.com/biz-cards-lego**

or

www.rexfeatures.com/search/?kw=lego+business+cards&search_newest.x=0&search_newest.y=0&search_newest=search_newest&iso=GBR&viah=Y&lkw=&stk=N&sft=&search_oldest.x=-1

Alternative URL: **tinyurl.com/biz-cards-lego2**

Career history

"History will be kind to me for I intend to write it."
Sir Winston Churchill (1874 - 1965), Prime Minister.

Your career history includes everything about what you've done in the past that is relevant to the jobs you are looking for. It includes such things as:

- formal education
- interests and hobbies
- key skills
- personal profile
- previous employment
- qualifications

To start the ball rolling, you need to do another exercise. Grab a couple of sheets of paper with the headings as shown below:

Current and past employers (including voluntary/unpaid work)

From (Date)	To (Date)	Company Name	Town/City (and Country if abroad)	Brief tasks and responsibilities	Achievements

Fig 12: Current and past employers

From the personal Inventory details you put together at page 8 you will be able to fill in quite a bit of the information. You should write down as much detail as you can about your previous employment and education.

At this stage, don't exclude anything. Even if you think something is totally irrelevant. Include everything you can from your personal inventory. This information will be needed for your CV *(page 45)* and application form template *(page 53)*.

Education (including any short non-certified courses)

From (Date)	To (Date)	Training or Educational organisation	Town/City (and Country if abroad)	Brief details of course	Qualifications and any achievements

Fig 13: Education and training courses

These experiences need to be documented and 'packaged' in such a way that prospective employers can instantly see what skills you have to offer. When job hunting, you must put together the following items before you start your search:

- **Portfolio** *(page 40)*
- **CV** *(page 45)*
- **Application form** *(page 51)*
- **Cover letter – draft** *(page 54)*
- **Letters of recommendation** *(page 56)*
- **List of referees** *(page 57)*

Your portfolio

A portfolio[11], in the job hunting sense, is an organised collection of documents that provides tangible evidence of your abilities, accomplishments, goals, qualifications, skills and even details of your character. It contains your best work and is clearly indexed for easy access. Your portfolio will never be complete because it should always be updated by including better samples of your work.

11 Part of your portfolio could also consist of physical objects which you may have created to demonstrate your skills. However, they need to be relevant to the jobs you're looking for.

It doesn't matter whether you're a student looking for your first job or if you've been working for a number of years. Your portfolio will prove to be a valuable asset that showcases your talents and experience. It's a handy way of backing up what you say in your job applications and interviews.

A well-prepared portfolio is guaranteed to give you the edge over many other job hunters. Most don't bother preparing one because it looks too much like hard work and they underestimate the power these have in influencing the decisions of interviewers.

One of the key benefits of having a portfolio to hand, during your interview, is that it illustrates the level of your strengths and verifies your experience in other not-so-proficient areas of expertise.

Please note:

Always bear in mind that samples of your work (included within your portfolio) may infringe on the confidentiality of your previous employer. If in doubt, leave them out. However, if their inclusion is likely to have a positive impact on the interview then blank out the confidential details.

Bear in mind your interviewer may be a direct competitor of your previous employer!

Beware

Beware 5: Confidentiality and your portfolio

An effective portfolio should include the following categories:

- **Achievements**
- **Aptitude for learning**
- **Biographical material**
- **Communication skills**
- **Community involvement**
- **Interpersonal skills**
- **Self-management skills**
- **Vocational skills**

On the following pages are some ideas of what you can include in your portfolio:

Achievements

Evidence of achievements shown in your CV, i.e. customer satisfaction and sales reports highlighting your successes. Also include letters (or memos) of recognition for your achievements and any thank you letters.

Aptitude for learning

Education certificates, university transcripts, scholarship awards, education grants, licences held (including driving) and examples of academic projects such as white papers or term papers.

Evidence of any education and training that you have undertaken. Even if a particular course of study doesn't strictly reflect the nature of the position you are applying for, still consider including it. With a little thought, you should be able to produce a list of transferable skills that you have gained from the training, i.e. benefits to prospective employer *(see pages 11 and 13)*.

Biographical material

CV (including the cover letter), hobbies, interests, sports, letters of introduction, personal history, passport, birth certificate, business cards, references, CRB check, letters of recommendation, testimonials, performance evaluations (reviews).

Communication skills

Articles or publications written (or co-written) by you and photographs of you conducting a presentation, lecture or training session.

Community involvement

Evidence of voluntary work including photographs, news clippings and letters of appreciation and any awards or recognition given.

Interpersonal skills

Evidence of leadership to include details of appointments and promotions, being elected as a team captain and employees representative or students union representative etc.

Self-management skills

Personal and career goals, self assessment (SWOT Analysis), evidence of time management skills, listing in professional directories (i.e. who's who lists), networking contacts, budgets or business plans you have been responsible for putting together[12], evidence of participation in professional organizations.

Vocational skills

Project samples that demonstrate your ability to perform a work-related task, work-related materials you have created, CD-ROMs or DVDs (you produced or appeared in), designs (such as brochures, flyers, publications) you created.

What is the simplest way to create your portfolio?

One of the easiest ways to accomplish this is to use a lever arch file, some plastic poly-pockets, blank white paper and some numerical dividers (numbered from 1 to 8 for example).

Even some of the larger supermarkets will stock these items. If not, a trip to your regular stationers will have what you want. They should cost you less than a fiver.

Fig 14: Basic portfolio creation materials

Create the contents page with the headings like those shown on page 41.

12 Be aware of confidentiality issues – see page 41.

Career Portfolio

Contents

Item	Section
Achievements	1
Aptitude For Learning	2
Biographical Material	3
Communication Skills	4
Community Involvement	5
Interpersonal Skills	6
Self-Management Skills	7
Vocational Skills	8

Fig 15: Sample portfolio contents sheet

Tips

You don't need expensive folders for your portfolio. However, you should aim for a professional and tidy-looking finish. You could use something like a lever-arch file for this purpose.

If you do, why not make it more presentable by printing out a heading for the outer cover on A4 coloured card and gluing it centrally. You could even laminate a cover-sheet and stick it to the front cover of the lever arch file with double-sided adhesive tape.

Tip 6: Portfolio creation

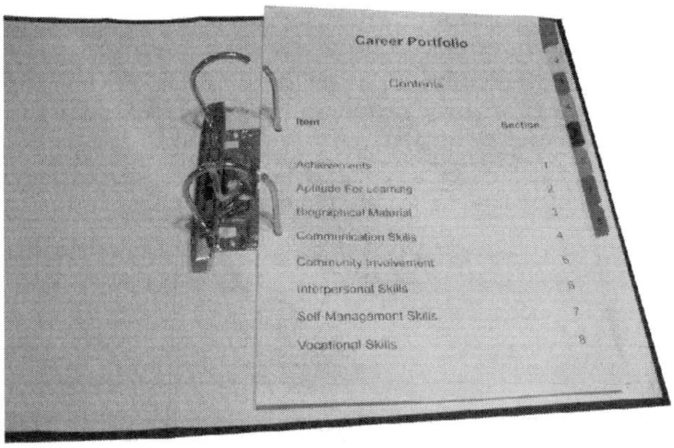

Fig 16: Newly constructed portfolio

Look through the eight broad topics shown in the sample portfolio contents sheet and collect as many items of evidence as you can. Start with any certificates you've been awarded with (whether for sports or academic achievements), your CV, birth certificate, driving licence etc. and place them into the appropriate sections.

To get your portfolio off to a quick start, you could also put together letters of recommendation (for use in the Biographical section). See page 56 for more information and tips.

Use one poly-pocket for each particular item. It is better to use photocopies rather than the original documents.

Don't spend too much time on perfection. This file will never be fully completed. Each time you produce better samples of your work, you will portray those in favour of the not so good ones..

Curriculum Vitae (Cvs)

> "Your CV has to be like a young plant in a tropical forest reaching up to the light. If it is to survive, it must use every tip and strategy that it can."
> *Max Eggert, Psychologist and author.*[13]

Types of CVs

Your CV is your opportunity to make that all-important good first impression. This is the single most-important document that leads to you getting your foot in the door to your new job.

13 Author of "Perfect CV", (2007).

Despite what you have previously understood about CVs, they are no more than an advertisement for **your services**. Indeed, you are selling your services to a prospective employer for a weekly or monthly salary. In simple terms, this 'advert' needs three ingredients to perform its job well:

- **highlight relevant skills for the job being applied for**
- **attract the hiring manager's attention**
- **create a great impression of you**

However, these won't guarantee a job. Their purpose is to capture the attention of the firm's hiring manager sufficiently enough to get you to the interview stage of the job hunt.

A great CV will get you to the top of the candidates pile. The first step is to choose the type of CV that best suits the purpose.

All CVs are not the same. The basic templates are different and you should be aware of this before you write your own. There are four types of CVs that you need to be acquainted with:

- **Chronological**
- **Functional (or skills-led)**
- **Targeted (or combination)**
- **Europass**

Chronological *(page 124)*

A chronological CV is the most common one in use. It lists your work history first, starting with your most recent job and working backwards through to the earlier ones. It provides an employer with a snapshot of your work history. That's why this CV is very popular with employers and recruiters. It's easy for them to check for any gaps in your career. If there are any unexplained gaps then you are unlikely to get short-listed for an interview.

Functional *(page 126)*

If you haven't had much work experience, you would be wise to use a functional CV. This is a great way to focus on the skills that distinguishes you from the majority of other applicants.

This CV focuses on your skills rather then your work experience. You may also consider choosing this one if you are changing careers or if you have large gaps in your employment history. An excellent CV for first time job hunters.

Targeted *(page 128)*

This is the most difficult one to use because you need to update it for every individual job you apply for. Although you should make minor adjustments to nearly every CV you send out, you really do need to put in some extra work for this one.

In a targeted CV, you showcase your skills that are relevant to the position you are applying for. If your skill set does not match the job requirements, then this CV will be a complete waste of time and effort on your part.

Europass

This is one of the least-known CV's and is one that you should know about if you're considering working elsewhere in Europe (if not, then skip this part). Some European companies stipulate in their job ads that a Europass CV is required. If so, then you can get more information on-line at:

> europass.cedefop.europa.eu/europass/home/vernav/Europasss+Documents/Europass+CV.csp
>
> *Alternative URL:* **tinyurl.com/Europass-CV**

If the job ad doesn't mention the need for one of these then don't try to impress a potential employer with one. Because Europass CVs are relatively uncommon, the chances are some employers have never heard of them before let alone seen one!

Main components of a CV

Personal details

No heading is needed for this but you should include your full name and contact details (postal address, telephone, mobile, fax and email address) giving many options for the prospective employer to contact you.

Personal profile

This usually consists of about two or three sentences which is written in the 'third person' (i.e. as if someone else wrote about you). It should highlight your strengths that mirror the requirements of the job *(See page 136 for a list to get you started).*

Key skills

This is normally a bulleted list of your skills that are relevant to the job you are looking for. You can get some inspiration from the Jobs 4 U website *(see the section below on Career/employment history).*

Career/employment history

List your previous jobs in reverse date order (latest job first) and give details such as the name and town/city of the employer, the job title (which can be put as a subheading using bold type). To the left of the heading will be the dates of employment. Beneath the heading you will insert the responsibilities of the job and any achievements you can think of to make you stand out from the crowd.

If you're stuck for something to say that would grab the prospective employer's attention then go to the Jobs 4 U website and have a look at the nearest job family to the one's listed in your CV:

www.connexions-direct.com/jobs4u/index.cfm?pid=2

Alternative URL: **tinyurl.com/Jobs4U-Database**

At the website, select a job family and browse specific jobs. You'll find plenty of information but you need to condense the responsibilities down to suit the jobs you did. Also see the sections on Job Research *(page 61)* and your list of current and previous employers *(page 39).*

Qualifications/memberships

List any academic qualifications, vocational qualifications and memberships that are relevant to the job you're applying for.

The educational listing you produced includes your qualifications *(page 40).*

Education and training

This is where you will list any academic and vocational training in reverse date order. The layout is similar to 'Career/Employment History' except that you'll insert the name of the training/educational establishment instead of the employer's name. You will also substitute the responsibilities/achievements with details of the training/course. This information can be gleaned from your list of educational achievements *(page 40).*

Interests

A prospective employer will want to see that you're an all-rounder and that you do have a life outside normal working hours. Here you'll put together a brief summary of your hobbies, interests, sports etc. Where possible try and show that you are reasonably fit both in body and mind. For example, swimming or walking shows that you keep yourself physically fit. Crosswords, reading and chess show that you exercise your mind. Doing some voluntary work for charity etc. shows some community involvement (i.e. helping others and being selfless).

So even from this underused section of the CV, a prospective employer can see another side of you which also grabs their attention on you.

Take another look at the section on 'Brainstorming your personal inventory' *(page 8)*.

Tips

Make a back up copy of your CV every time you produce a new one.

A simple yet effective way to do this is to send a copy of each version to your own email account. That way, you'll have a back up of each version even when you don't have access to your computer.

If you run out of CVs when visiting recruitment agencies, you could always ask them if you can access your email account to print off a copy.

Tip 7: Backing up your CVs

On-line services for CV production

There are a number of reputable on-line services that can help you create and produce a very professional-looking CV.

Here's some you might find of use:

www.resumizer.com

www.niceresume.com

www.pongoresume.com

www.skillcraze.com

Printing and presentation

Although your CV has been completed, you are not quite done yet. It needs to be printed out and ready out to send to prospective employers.

Here's some ways to give your CV that professional look:

- Go to your local stationers (i.e. Staples) and have your CV printed out from a flash drive[14]. The store assistants can advise you of the correct paper for printing. This removes any guess-work out of printing your CV. However it will cost you a little extra money for good quality paper.
- You can print your CV at home. Make sure that your printer's ink cartridge is full so that you have a clean and crisp print. You will need some good quality paper (a heavier weight than normal photocopying paper is best). Aim for somewhere in the region of 100 – 120 gsm[15]. When buying the paper, have a look at the labels to ensure that you have the right weight. White or cream coloured paper are appropriate for most CVs.
- You could print off one high quality master copy at home and have it photocopied when needed at any stationers, your local library, job centre or recruitment agency. However, bear in mind that you may not have control over the paper quality.

If you are printing CVs at home, you don't need many copies. You should always have about a dozen ready to take with you everywhere you go. Opportunities present themselves unexpectedly. For example, you might be out and see a job ad in a shop window or outside an recruitment agency. If you are socialising with a friend, it may well be that they know of someone who is looking for people with your skills. Whatever opportunity arises, you'll be at the ready with a copy of your CV.

The main reason for not printing out too many copies is that your CV will need adjusting from time to time to reflect the requirements of each job you apply for.

14 A flash drive is the size of a small penknife and stores your computer files. They can even be purchased from large supermarkets.

15 Abbreviation for grams per square metre which measures the weight of paper.

Tips

Use:

a laser printer whenever possible

high-quality stationery

cream or ivory-coloured paper

paper between 100 to 120 gsm in weight

Avoid:

heavy paper that can crease and damage the print

Tip 8: Recommended stationery for CVs

Application forms

Bear in mind that numerous employers prefer you to complete an application form rather than submit a CV. Don't ever be put off by this.

There are two methods of completing application forms:

On-line

When searching for jobs on-line, you will come across large company websites which require you to complete an on-line form. The most common mistake is to complete an one totally unprepared.

The best approach to this is to print off the questions and write your responses out by hand in the first instance. Once you have all the information together, go back on-line and transfer the information across.

You could make it easier on yourself by typing out your responses using a word processing software (even Notepad is more than adequate for this) then just copy and paste your response onto the on-line form.

Ensure you spell check the boxes before submitting the form. Many websites have a built in feature which spell-checks the information you type in. If not, go to page 35 to find out where you can download a free on-line spell checker.

Off-line

The off-line method is where you complete a physical form that may be downloaded from a website or requested directly from the company itself.

Many job hunters who request an application form either fail to send them off or, if they do, only make a half-hearted attempt to complete them.

Either way these job hunters are missing out on some great opportunities. This is excellent news for you. It means that there's relatively less competition for jobs where completed application forms are required.

Beware

Always:

Before completing one of these forms, take a photocopy and use this copy for rough work, making any corrections before transferring the details to the original form.

Read through the application form, paying particular attention as to whether black ink is required and whether capital letters are needed.

Never:

Never use the words "See Attached CV". The purpose of the application form is for the prospective employer to have a consistent layout and they don't have the time to flick through CVs as well as application forms!

Never leave any blank spaces otherwise the prospective employer may think you are either hiding something or you just forgot to fill it in. If something doesn't apply to you then write the words "Not Applicable" or "None" as appropriate.

Beware 6: Application form completion

There are good reasons why some companies insist on application forms - the main ones are:

- A familiar layout can make the initial filtering (or screening) process much faster.
- Checking whether an applicant has the desired skills or experience is much easier.
- Every applicant is treated equally (i.e. it doesn't matter how fancy a CV looks).
- If specific information is required from the applicant, it is easier to spot anything that is left out or if there are any inconsistencies with the overall application.
- Only applicants who are really serious about applying for the particular job will go through the trouble of completing the application form in such detail.

It is inevitable that you will come across job ads where you must complete an application form. So don't wait until the last minute before you respond. Just like you have a prepared CV at your disposal, you should also have an application form template that you can use. So here's a way to prepare yourself.

Application form template

Download a sample application form from the internet and print it out. Fill in the required information in pencil so that it can be erased and updated without having to re-write it completely. Ensure you complete the parts which ask you to write something about "why you feel you are suited to the job" or "why your skills and experience make you a suitable candidate" etc. Once completed, keep this template in a safe place with the master copies of your CV.

Tips

Open up your web browser and enter the following URL:

tinyurl.com/Application-Forms

A Google search page will open up which will list a number of UK Government websites where you can print off an application form. Click on any of the links down the left side of the page and download an application form. Once downloaded, open up the file with Adobe Acrobat Reader and print it out.

Enter your details onto the form as if you are applying for a specific type of job (i.e. the one you are conducting your job hunting on) and use this as your template for filling in future application forms.

If you are unable to open the downloaded files, you can get a copy of Acrobat Reader here:

www.adobe.com/products/acrobat/read step2.html

Alternative URL:
tinyurl.com/Acrobat-Reader

Tip 9: Downloading application form templates

Cover letters

A cover letter is needed to send out your CVs and application forms. Many employers will skip over CVs because they lack a well written cover letter.

The best way to create one is to imagine it as a script that introduces you to an audience. It is a short one-page introduction that gives a brief insight into the background and skills you have to offer. This is the place to convince a prospective employer to have a good look at your CV.

The biggest mistake job hunters make is to write just one cover letter and use it for every single job application. They might as well save themselves the bother (and postage) because there's a good chance it will be thrown out anyway.

Put it this way; If someone wrote a letter, duplicated it and sent a copy to you, would you really be interested? Of course not. Don't forget that a prospective employer will be judging you by your covering letter and if you don't make an effort to write a personalised one then it will be assumed that you won't make any effort to do the job properly if ever they hired you.

Hiring managers want to see some effort and creativeness put into the cover letters they receive. Having said that, there is no reason why you can't use a cover letter template and then tailor each one to the job that you're applying for. This will help your cover letter stand out and increase the odds of you being short-listed for an interview.

To customise a cover letter template you will need some basic information about each job. It is good job hunting practice to keep a copy of each job ad that you apply for. This will be a vital piece of information which you will refer to as you prepare your application for the job. It will be used in the **opening paragraph** of your covering letter i.e.:

> **"I am writing in response to your advertisement regarding the post of Retail Manager as shown in the Daily Echo of 15th January 2010."**

Always include the job details showing where you saw this ad because the company may have a number of different vacancies on the go and it will ensure that your application gets the appropriate attention it deserves.

If there is a contact name on the ad, you must ensure the covering letter is addressed to that person by name. If there isn't, phone the company and ask for the name of the person who your application should be directed to. Many job hunters will address their applications to an appointment, whereas you have shown initiative and personalised your cover letter which will make your application stand out from the crowd.

Your cover letter needs a proper structure *(see page 131)*.

Tips

Whenever possible, address your letter to a specific individual by name. Contact the company to find out the name if necessary. If you do not have the company's phone number then look them up in the yellow pages:

www.yell.com

Be sure you use the correct spelling (particularly if it's an unusual name) and if the person you should write to is female make sure you know whether she prefers to be known as Miss, Mrs or Ms.

> Get your letter to fit on one side of A4 paper.
>
> Use a formal business layout for your letter that shows your address and that of the recipient.
>
> Use 'Yours sincerely' to sign off (only use 'Yours faithfully' if you have addressed the letter as 'Dear Sir' or 'Dear Madam' etc.).

Tip 10: Cover letters

While we are on the subject of letters, there are two types of letter which people get confused over. These are 'Recommendation Letters' (or **Letters of Recommendation)** and 'Letters of Reference' (normally known as **References**).

A letter of recommendation is a letter in which the writer puts together an assessment of the qualities and skills of a person they are recommending. It is usual for them to be written generically and addresses to "To Whom It May Concern" etc. They are ideal for interviews where they can reinforce the candidate's claims.

On the other hand, a reference can be in the form of a letter but usually the prospective employer will send the referee a standard form to complete. This makes it easy for the interviewers to cross-compare other candidates for the job. Whether the recommendation is by letter or form, it will be addressed to a specific person or department.

Letters of recommendation

Letters of recommendation are very useful because they act as generic references which help to convince the prospective employer to employ (or at least short-list) you for the job. These should be placed in your portfolio and made available at the interview. If the prospective employer needs to make a hiring decision quickly, they can be assured you are the right person for the job.

To get you started, here's some samples:

> businessmajors.about.com/od/samplerecommendations/tp/TopRecLetters.htm
>
> *Alternative URL:* **tinyurl.com/Rec-Ltrs**

By planning ahead, you will have a distinct advantage over any other candidate by having these documents handy. So how do you get letters of recommendation?

Go through your networking list, particularly your previous managers and ask them to put together a simple letter of recommendation for you.

Tips

If you are in a hurry to put together a draft letter of recommendation, go to:

> boxfreeconcepts.com/generators/letmascproc.html
>
> *Alternative URL:*
> **tinyurl.com/Rec-Letter**

You'll be able to produce one within a couple of minutes Just copy the result and paste it straight into a word-processor for final editing.

Tip 11: Letters of recommendation

It is a good idea to draft the letter yourself and then send it out to your business contacts for signing. By doing this, they can make any amendments necessary and return a signed copy back within a couple of days. Be sure to enclose a self-addressed envelope to make this easier for them.

References

No matter what job you are applying for, professional references will be asked for. Always ensure you have at least three people available to provide references for when you are short-listed for a job.

These referees should not be personal friends of yours but people you have had a professional relationship with. They can be previous supervisors or even co-workers if needed.

Unfortunately, some companies have a policy where they don't allow their employees to give references for ex-employees. In cases like this, it would be best to ask other ex-employees if they would be willing to act as a referee.

Even if you did voluntary work in the past, this can still count as far as references are concerned. Just ask one of your former colleagues (preferably a supervisor) to act as a referee. These people have seen your work ethic, can talk about your time management and dedication to the job.

Once you've got permission from at least three people (the more the better) be sure you have the following information at hand:

- **Referee's full name (including whether Mr, Miss, Ms or Mrs etc.)**
- **Job title of referee**
- **Organisation they work for (or worked for)**
- **Relationship of referee (e.g. line manager)**
- **Address (could be home address)**
- **Email address (if applicable)**
- **Telephone No**
- **Fax No (if applicable)**
- **Whether the referee can be contacted prior to an interview**

If a prospective employer asks whether the referee can be contacted before the interview, you really should consider saying no. If you attended a number of interviews and have not accepted the job offer, your referees will soon get tired of writing references for you. Therefore it is better that they are only contacted by the prospective employers when absolutely necessary (i.e. after the interview).

Part II

The Job Hunt

The job hunt

> "Choose a job you love, and you will never have to work a day in your life."
> *Confucius (551 – 479 BC), Philosopher.*

Your CV should now be completed and you've got copies handy. Now the real 'journey' begins. There is an old saying that "looking for a job is a job in itself". It's quite true. Job hunting cannot be done half-heartedly. You need to put in the same effort (if not more) in looking for a job as you would if actually working for a living.

Although this process takes a bit of dedication on your part, if you do it systematically then it will be so much easier. You really do need to regularly set aside some time each day for job hunting.

The majority of people who say that they cannot find a job, are usually the ones who don't invest the time looking or they are going the wrong way about it.

Often, you will not know if the job you're interested in is really the one for you. Only when you get to the interview will you get a clearer picture of the job and the people you'd be working for. That is why you will want to devote the time to finding as many jobs as possible to apply for.

This is why you need to look at job hunting as if it were a real job. By doing so, you will take it more seriously and be successful in landing the most suitable one for you.

Preliminary research

Some research is essential before applying for jobs:

- **Job research**
- **Company research**

Job research

Without question, some research is necessary unless you want to settle for a mundane job. Many job seekers assume they should only consider the same type of jobs that they've done before. The worrying thing is that in most cases they probably hated the work they did before!

In contrast, you are a job hunter who keeps your options open. You will be assessing your skills, experiences and personality profile to look for a wide range of suitable work.

Collect together all of the lists you made in the Self-awareness section *(page 8)*:

- **Personal inventory**
- **Personality profile**
- **Minimum income requirements**

Now go to the Connexions Jobs 4 U database:

www.connexions-direct.com/jobs4u/index.cfm?pid=2

Alternative URL: **tinyurl.com/Jobs4U-Database**

Browse the job families and search for the types of work you believe you will enjoy. Each time you find one, take a look at what the job requires and see if they match your experiences and skills. Remember you are not necessarily looking for the same work as before but widening your horizons to other industries where your skills are also valued.

After spending a couple of hours on this website, put together a list of suitable jobs and print out the job specifications.

You will also be using these specifications as a basis for writing speculative letters to potential employers. Use them in conjunction with your job hunt for the hidden job market *(page 70)*.

The list of suitable job titles will make your job hunting more efficient since you have selected the job roles based on your own personal inventory and personality profiles. Use these lists to search through job ads on the Internet, newspapers and local recruitment agencies.

Company research

There is no real need to do too much in-depth company research before you've been short-listed for an interview. You wouldn't be able to squeeze the time in with your other job hunting activities anyway! However, if you are sending out speculative letters then it is essential that you seek out around twenty to thirty companies at a time and dig out some basic details. You will need to find the following information about each one:

- **Full company name and address**
- **Their contact information**
- **Hiring manager's name**[16]
- **Their products and services**

The above items are necessary because you need to include certain elements within your speculative letter.

Where to look for job leads

There are many places to find job leads. The old way of going from door to door and asking business owners/managers whether they are hiring, may seem to be a thing of the past. However, if you are serious about finding a job, you may consider this especially if you are looking for a retail job. Many shops will have a sign in the window (or on the customer services notice board) if they have vacancies anyway.

However, the majority of your job hunting can be done from the comfort of your own home. If you have a computer with Internet access, you can do as much as 90% of your job hunting on-line.

If you have access to local and national newspapers (either delivered to your door or via the local library) then you must obviously make a habit of going through the jobs sections.

Local recruitment agencies

Local recruitment agencies have an important part to play in any successful job hunt. Remember, you want to leverage your time and, if you can get many people helping you to find a job, then your task is all that much easier.

You'll eventually have to get out of the house and do some footwork. But first, go to the Yellow Pages website:

www.yell.com

and search for the following:

Careers advice

Employment Agencies

16 You may have to phone their company and get this information. Be subtle and don't tell them why you want to know in case they just turn round and say they are not advertising at the moment etc.

Job Centres

Recruitment Consultants

Contact the agencies nearest to where you live to find out if they deal with the type of jobs you're looking for. If any don't, just cross those off the list and visit the ones a little further afield.

Take sufficient CVs with you to hand out. Also, make sure you take a copy of your completed application form template *(page 53)* because some agencies will ask you to complete one of their registration forms that request similar information. Don't forget to take the following, with you, wherever you go:

- **A6 notebook and pen** *(page 10)*
- **business cards** *(page 37)*

On-line job sites

The world has certainly embraced the Internet, particularly when it comes to job hunting. On-line job sites have now become one of the most popular options for job hunters everywhere. There are so many different job sites to search on – Monster, Career Builder, Jobsite and Fish4Jobs are amongst the most popular.

Here's a list to get you started:

(1) MULTI-SECTOR

All The Top Bananas
www.allthetopbananas.com

Career Builder
www.careerbuilder.co.uk

Fish 4 Jobs
www.fish4.co.uk/jobs/sector

Get Me Off The Dole
www.GetMeOffTheDole.com/Search

Hot Recruit
www.hotrecruit.com

Jobcentre Plus
www.Jobcentre Plus.gov.uk/Internet/setLocale.do?country=GB&language=en&page=/initialise.do
Alternative URL: tinyurl.com/jobcentre

Job Quest
www.job-quest.net

Jobs Ac.UK
www.jobs.ac.uk

Jobserve
www.jobserve.com

Jobsite
www.jobsite.co.uk

London Careers Net
www.londoncareers.net

Milk Round
www.milkround.com

Monster
www.monster.co.uk

Planet Recruit
www.planetrecruit.com

Reed
www.reed.co.uk

Total Jobs
www.totaljobs.com

Work Thing
www.workthing.com

SPECIFIC

two websites provide an extensive list of ...t agencies and job sites which cater for specific ...tries:

Agency Central
www.agencycentral.co.uk

Agency Seeker
www.agency-seeker.co.uk

(3) DISABILITIES

Although the above websites cater for people with disabilities, the following offer more specialist advice.

Jobability
www.jobability.com

Disability Jobsite
www.disabilityjobsite.co.uk

(4) EX HM FORCES

Pathfinder International
www.pathfinderinternational.co.uk

Career Transition Partnership
www.ctp.org.uk

There are several advantages to using on-line job sites. The main one is that there's so many job listings on each site. This saves a great deal of time whilst job hunting. By typing in a few keywords relating to the job you're looking for, you can filter out any unsuitable ones. Instead of searching each of the sites every single day, you can register with them and get notified, by email, when your preferred jobs are listed on their website.

Another advantage of using on-line job sites is that prospective employers can also seek you out. You don't always have to find every single job opening yourself. The way to do this is to look for those job sites which allow you to post your profile onto their database. In this way you can make your CV searchable by prospective employers, therefore increasing the likelihood of getting a job that much sooner.

However, there are some disadvantages to using job sites, particularly if you use them as your only source of finding jobs. You may be competing with several other applicants for every position you apply for. Because of their popularity, there are thousands of people logging into them every day to search.

Newspapers

One of the tried and tested ways of job hunting is by scanning through the newspaper ads. Many prospective employers, particularly the smaller businesses, prefer this method because they don't feel comfortable with posting their job vacancies on-line. Because of this, many job vacancies that appear in the local and national newspapers won't appear on-line. Hence you should always use these two sources in tandem.

Below is a list of some of the most popular national newspapers with links to their jobs pages:

Daily Mail
Uses Jobsite *(See MULTI-SECTOR – page 64)*

Financial Times
www.exec-appointments.com

Guardian
jobs.guardian.co.uk

Telegraph
jobs.telegraph.co.uk

The Independent
Uses London Careers Net *(See MULTI-SECTOR – page 64)*

The Sun
jobs.thesun.co.uk

Times
business.timesonline.co.uk/tol/business/career_and_jobs

Alternative URL: tinyurl.com/times-jobs

Here's a very handy (and regularly updated) resource that includes local on-line newspapers:

On-line Newspapers.Com

England (Locations A-K)

www.onlinenewspapers.com/englanda-k.htm

England (Locations L-Z)

www.onlinenewspapers.com/englandl-z.htm

Scotland

www.onlinenewspapers.com/scotland.htm

Wales

www.onlinenewspapers.com/wales.htm

Overseas

www.onlinenewspapers.com

One of the drawbacks with using newspaper ads for job hunting is that the process takes longer than their on-line counterparts. You will need to send off a postal application in the traditional way. However, if you have your CV and covering letter template ready then this really shouldn't be quite so much of a problem.

Many companies, that place newspapers ads, also place CVs into a database so that they can search for keywords from promising candidates. Once your CV is received, it is scanned onto their system. This is one reason why it takes longer than on-line applications.

Search engines

There are quite a few search engines on the Internet which can be used for job hunting. Google seems to be the most popular because it's index contains more listings than any other search engine. The URL for Google is:

www.google.co.uk

If, for example, you are looking for a job as a Van Driver in London then you should enter the following in the search box:

"van driver" job london

A search for this term will uncover thousands of web pages. Unfortunately many of them will be too old and outdated to be of any use (in some cases web pages advertising jobs have been known to be over a year old!) To avoid this, click on the "Advanced Search" link, found next to the "Search" button. Scroll down the next page until you see this link:

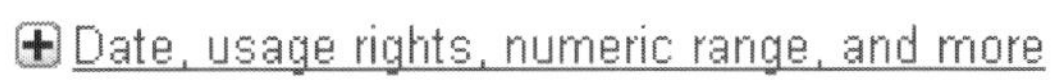

There's a few options including this one:

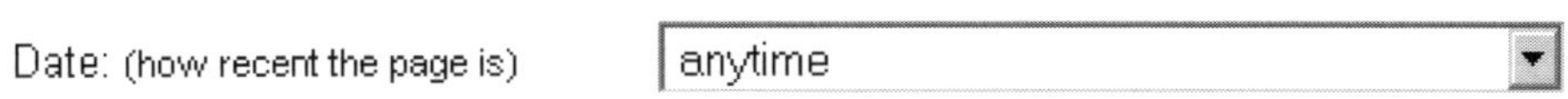

Click on the down-pointing arrow and change "anytime" for "past 24 hours" or "past week" and then click on the "Advanced Search" button.

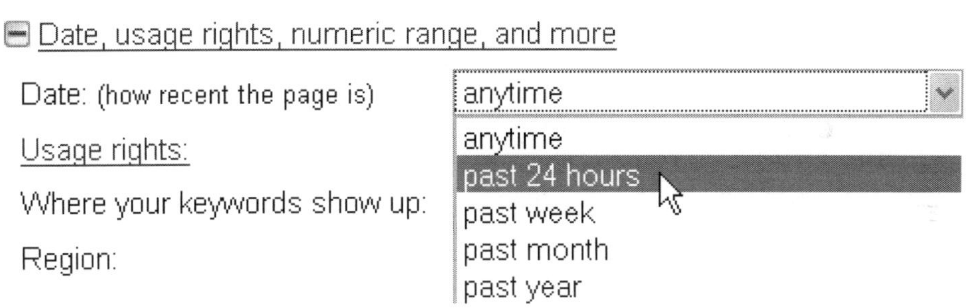

Fig 17: Filtering out older web pages

Other top search engines/directories to try out are:

Ask Jeeves

uk.ask.com

Bing

www.bing.com/?cc=uk

Dmoz

www.dmoz.org/Regional/Europe/United_Kingdom

Alternative URL: tinyurl.com/Open-Dir

Get me Off The Dole

www.GetMeOffTheDole.Com/search-engine

Surf Canyon

search.surfcanyon.com/search

Yahoo

uk.yahoo.com

Hidden job market

A considerable number of jobs do go unadvertised. Because of this it's difficult to pin down exactly how many. Estimates are wide ranging and are anything from 50% to 80% (average of about 65%). Let's round this down to 60% to be even more cautious. This being the case then somewhere in the region of only 40% of jobs are actually advertised!

According to the UK Government:

> "The number of vacancies in the three months to November 2009 was 432,000"[17]
> *Office for National Statistics*

If this figure is correct then we can make an informed guess as to how many jobs were actually available in the three months to November 2009:

Advertised jobs	432,000
Hidden job market	648,000
Estimated total vacancies	**1,080,000**

This gives us an idea of how many jobs are available. If the above numbers are anything to go by then you can see why it is well well worth

17 www.statistics.gov.uk/cci/nugget.asp?ID=12

venturing into this 'hidden' job market and gain an advantage over the majority of job seekers.

Some of the places to look for these hidden jobs are:

Job fairs *(page 71)*
Networking *(pages 36 and 73)*
News *(pages 73 and 86)*
On-line communities *(page 74)*
Planning applications *(page 76)*
Professional organisations *(pages 77 and 155)*
Self-promotion *(page 78)*
Top employers *(pages 82 and 142)*
Yellow pages *(page 83)*

Many jobs go unadvertised for a number of reasons. For example:

- **the jobs are offered to employees first**
- **they prefer to take on someone that has been recommended**
- **they receive so many speculative job letters they don't need to advertise**
- **to avoid paying huge advertising costs**

Of course there are many more reasons but I'm sure you get the idea.

Job fairs

Many companies taking part in job fairs are regularly looking for new talent and may not always place job advertisements. Some tend to put a lot of effort into a mass recruitment campaign and then short-list suitable candidates. However, they sometimes have the odd vacancy outside the recruitment surge. Therefore a quick search for these companies will uncover some very receptive ones.

To find the names of organisations that use job fairs, go on-line to Google:

www.google.co.uk

Enter the following search term in the text box:

uk job-fair

In the search results you'll discover forthcoming job fairs being held around the UK. Take a look through this listing and select the names of large companies who are recruiting people for the jobs you are after. If you don't mind relocating, then send them a speculative job letter *(sample on page 140)*. However, if you want to remain in your local area then add your town or county on to the end of the search phrase:

uk job-fair london

uk job-fair hampshire

Remember to replace the words "**london**" and "**hampshire**" with your own town or county.

Don't just restrict your job fairs research to ones which are taking place in the future. You'll find organisations that participated in previous job fairs may still be on the look out for new employees.

Make a list of the companies that have previously taken part and get hold of the hiring manager's name. Send speculative job letters enclosing your CV. They may not be looking for anyone at that moment but will normally keep your details on file until a vacancy arises. You could well be sending your speculative job letter at a time when they are looking for someone but haven't got round to advertising the post.

Tips

When searching for local or county-wide job fairs, make a note in your diary to visit them. When you do, take plenty of CVs and business cards with you *(page 37)*.

While you are there, get as much information about each company (even if they don't *seem* to be looking for people with your talents right now). Get the names of the hiring managers too. When you get back home, send out some speculative job letters.

Tip 12: Job fairs

Networking

This is one of the most under-used job hunting strategies. Networking (in the job hunting sense) is all about keeping in touch with other people with a view to uncovering job leads.

Your networking should begin with your own circle of friends. Make sure they're all aware you're looking for a job. Ask them if they can recommend anything. You'll be surprised at some of the responses you get. Have another look at the tip on the use of email signatures at page 27.

Bring up this topic up in future conversations with them so they won't forget. Just ask them if they'd discuss the matter with their friends too. If each of your friends asked their friends, the chances of finding work will increase exponentially[18].

If you haven't already done so, go through the section on "Networking Lists" *(page 36)*.

News

Listening to, or reading, the latest news can uncover some really great opportunities. Obviously if you hear of a company opening up new premises nearby, you'll instantly realise that they'll need new staff. Many job seekers, rather than sending out a speculative letter, will wait until they see an 'official' job ad from the company. Unfortunately these people have completely 'missed the boat' and now find themselves competing with considerably more candidates than they would otherwise have.

Sometimes you may hear about a company that's been landed with a huge contract or order. This means theyhave at least four options:

- **give overtime to existing staff**
- **outsource some of the work to other businesses**
- **take on more staff**
- **take on new contractors**

There's at least a 50-50 chance that they'll take a serious look at your speculative letter and CV (i.e. as a contractor or permanent staff). So don't wait for the job ads to appear – go on and get your speculative letter out that very day. A sample speculative letter is shown on page 140.

---

18 i.e. If you personally know 50 people and each of them told 50 others then your message would get round to 2,500 people!

Apart from watching TV and reading the newspapers, you can get the latest news from the Internet. One way is to browse through the news articles listed on Google:

news.google.co.uk/news/search?
aq=f&pz=1&cf=all&ned=uk&hl=en&q=jobs

Alternative URL: **tinyurl.com/Google-Job-News**

You can narrow down the search by clicking on one of the options shown (i.e. **Past day** or **Past week**):

On-line communities

Newsgroups

Typically, a Newsgroup is where a number of Internet 'discussions' take place on various topics (including job hunting). These text-based topics are formed into groups and accessible by anyone. You may need to formally join a particular group to access the discussions but they are usually free.

The following Newsgroups are amongst the most popular:

Google Groups

groups.google.co.uk

Yahoo Groups

uk.groups.yahoo.com

The downside is that there's a lot of 'junk' put on these groups so you really should to do a search using keywords like **jobs uk wanted** followed by the industry, i.e.:

jobs uk wanted engineering

You may need to experiment a little to find useful leads though.

Forums

A Forum is similar to a newsgroup but it is far more structured and better moderated. They are well-worth looking at. The best way to find a forum, on the Internet, is to go to Google and type in the following search term:

uk [industry][19] forum

Blogs

There are thousands and thousands of blogs on every conceivable subject imaginable. However, there are two quick ways to find some useful blogs to get the latest posts on your industry:

(1) **Go to Google** (www.google.co.uk)

Enter this search term:

uk [industry][19] blog

(2) **Go to Technorati (**technorati.com)

Enter your search term (i.e. your industry etc.) and select the "Blog" button rather than the "Posts":

Twitter

Although Twitter is good for self-promotion *(page 78)*, it is also a very useful tool for 'listening in' on conversations. A little experimentation is needed to uncover some great leads. Go to Twitter Search:

search.twitter.com

---

19 Just replace **[industry]** with your own industry, i.e. **uk engineering forum** or **uk engineering blog**

. . . and try out the following searches:

looking for a receptionist[20]
looking for a reliable person
looking for a local
we have a vacancy for
we have an opening for
we urgently need a

Beware

Please note:

If you're not careful you may end up spending too much of your time with on-line communities - they can become quite addictive!

So take a look at some of these methods and decide for yourself which to focus on.

Beware 7: On-line communities – time consuming

Planning permission

Organisations that are expanding their business (or moving into new premises) may need to obtain planning permission before going ahead. If these organisations are going to recruit new employees then they'll do so soon after permission has been granted.

You can freely search the on-line records of organisations who applied for such permission by going to local council websites. To find their web address go to Google:

www.google.co.uk

and use the following search criteria:

"Planning application search" london site:.gov.uk

Remember to replace the word 'london' with your town, city or county.

---

20 Change this for the job role you're looking for.

Once you've clicked on a link, you may be taken to an on-line form where you can conduct your search. The simplest way is to search by date since you have no other information to go by at this stage. Try searching for the past six months or so to start with.

Your search results will include all planning permissions so you will need to browse through them to get information about companies who may be expanding.

If you don't have much luck, try going back to Google and using the following search instead:

london list of planning applications site:.gov.uk filetype:pdf

Or try this alternative URL:

tinyurl.com/Planning-Apps

Again, ensure you replace the word 'london' with your local town or county.

This will bring up lists of documents in pdf format. You will need Acrobat Reader installed on your computer to access these files. If you don't have Acrobat Reader, you can download the latest version from the Internet:

get.adobe.com/uk/reader

If you're unsuccessful with your on-line searches, you can always visit your local council offices (or public library) and ask to see the public planning applications.

Professional Organisations

Keeping in touch with professional organisations within your industry will unearth some excellent opportunities. Page 155 gives a list of websites of the main British professional organisations. You might discover that more than one of the listed organisations are relevant to your industry. If that's the case, so much the better.

Your local library and larger newsagents are good places to find a selection of trade magazines *(also see page 163)*. You need to keep yourself updated on the latest industry news (you may be asked questions relating to this at your interview) as well as finding out about new jobs.

A relatively unknown source for many job hunters is the **Writers and Artists Yearbook**. Libraries and larger bookshops will usually have copies.

When you get hold of the book, look through the listing of magazines and pick out any which apply to your industry. If your local library or magazine shop don't have a copy of the magazine, listed in the Yearbook, you could contact the publishers and request one. Sometimes you can get lucky and they'll send you a free one if you tell them you are interested in becoming a subscriber!

Tips

The Writers and Artists Yearbook have their own website where you can register for free and search the database for magazines. Go to the following URL, enter your industry in the box marked "Full text search" and select "Magazines UK and Ireland" in the Category box:

> **www.writersandartists.co.uk**
> **search-listings**
>
> *Alternative URL:*
> **tinyurl.com/WAA-YearBook**

At the search results, click on any web page links to the magazine website. Many of the websites will have industry news and even a jobs page.

Tip 13: Writers and Artists Yearbook

On page 163 there is also a listing of popular trade magazines.

Self-promotion

As well as seeking out prospective employers through the 'Hidden Job Market' you should also consider self promotion tactics that get the employers to come to you. Some are more effective than others and this will largely depend on the type of job you are after. The following is a list of ideas to get you thinking:

Print and distribute flyers

Get some flyers printed and distributed in places where your prospective employers are located (i.e. industrial or retail parks, shops etc.).

Blogging

You could set up a blog (i.e. **Wordpress**: **www.wordpress.com** or **Blogger**: **www.blogger.com**) that's related to your line of expertise and post weekly or twice-weekly tips and articles. Make sure you have a way of getting people to contact you by email.

The URL of the blog can be inserted in the header of your CV to attract more interest. If you don't have the inclination or time to set up a blog then I recommend that you consider setting up a Linkedin account *(see below)*.

Press Release

If you have a blog, you can submit occasional press-releases by mail and on-line to get more attention. Below are a couple of sources to get you started:

Press Box

www.pressbox.co.uk/contpr2.htm

Business Link

www.businesslink.gov.uk/bdotg/action/detail?type=RESOURCES&itemId=1073790963

Alternative URL: **tinyurl.com/BizLink-PR**

Twitter

Set up a Twitter account (**www.twitter.com**) and insert a link to your blog. Send out a couple of short messages (or Tweets) each day that are of interest to people in your industry. Whenever you post a new article to your blog you can also send out a Tweet with a link to your latest blog article. If you're new to Twitter, you'll find the following resources very helpful:

www.commoncraft.com/Twitter

help.twitter.com/forums

Linkedin

Linkedin (**www.linkedin.com**) is one of the most widely used and influential business networking sites on the Internet. Even the likes of Richard Branson and Alan Sugar have used it! If you want some helpful tips on how to set up a profile, go to:

jobsearch.about.com/od/networking/a/linkedinprofile.htm

Alternative URL: **tinyurl.com/linkedin-p**

Ecademy

Ecademy is a prominent UK networking site for like-minded business people.

> "Ecademy enables business people to connect through online networking using social media tools, at business networking events and 1-2-1 meetings - a community that connects, refers and helps one another."
> *(Quoted from the Ecademy website)*

To find out more, go to:

www.ecademy.com

Business Cards

Get some business cards printed and carry them around with you. If you do have a blog and Twitter account, insert the URLs on the card *(See page 37)*.

Video

If good presentation skills are a key part of your career (i.e. managerial, sales, training etc.), you could set up a Youtube account (**www.youtube.com**). Once set up, you then submit a video of yourself (or a narrated powerpoint presentation and converted to video) to Youtube. The URL of your blog can be included in the video, and description, to get more attention.

This list should give you some ideas on creative ways to get your name out to potential employers. Just one word of caution though. Don't give out unnecessary personal details on the Internet unless you are satisfied that such information is kept confidential. Your main objective is to grab the attention of potential employers – not give everyone your life history!

Real-life examples

There are a number of creative ways in which job hunters are currently promoting themselves to capture the attention of prospective employers. Here's three unusual ones:

Car Magnet

Some job hunters have registered with a site called **On The Way Resume**. After paying a small fee for magnetic car stickers, job hunters stick them to the side of their cars. Potential employers would look at the details, look at you and hopefully go to the website and enter the job hunter's reference number. There, they can check out the resume (i.e. CV) and get in touch.

> "In today's economy, job seekers have to be willing to stand out from the crowd and make it simple for potential employers to find them. Having an On The Way Resume sticker on your vehicle shows a level of initiative that potential employers like to see and helps employers quickly determine if your qualifications are a fit with a current opening at their company."
> *Shawn Hermanson, Founder of On The Way Resume*

It's only a matter of time before this concept catches on here in the UK. There's nothing to stop a job hunter like you from putting up a website with a CV page, and fixing a magnetic sticker to your own car. You can check out the **On The Way Resume** website from here:

onthewayresume.com

Billboard

Gordon Flynn, an enterprising job hunter, got in touch with a billboard agency and talked them into letting him borrow a 6 metre x 3 metre board situated in in Tottenham Court Road, London.

After being unemployed for 6 months and finding that his CV was one of around five hundred submitted for a position, he knew he had to do something innovative. He came up with the idea that promoting himself on advertising hoardings and billboards in London would be the ideal platform to get noticed by the nations managers and directors.

On Job Seekers Allowance there is little left at the end of each week to pay for expensive advertising, so he wrote to a director at JC Decaux, who are Europe's No.1 for billboards, asking if he could use one of their boards for free to get himself noticed. To his delight, they accepted and assigned him an account manager wishing him luck.

He chose an easy to remember domain name[21], built a website to host his CV and designed the poster himself.

Classified advertising

Neville Keithley, an unemployed Managing Director, placed a large personal classified ad in the Daily Telegraph in April 2009. He was 47 years old when he was made redundant.

> "I have negotiated with headhunters, talked to people in the industry, networked; you name it I have done it. I think we are in different times and you need to do something totally different in to get yourself noticed."
> *Neville Keithley, quoted in the Daily Telegraph of 9th April 2009.*

You can read more about Neville Keithley[22] on The Daily Telegraph's website:

> www.telegraph.co.uk/finance/jobs/5159987/Unemployed-executive-Neville-Keithleys-gisajob-advert-in-The-Daily-Telegraph-throws-up-new-leads.html
>
> *Alternative URL:* **tinyurl.com/Neville-Keithley**

Top employers

As part of your overall job hunting strategy you should consider working for one of the top employers. However, there are many interpretations of what a top employer is. To some, a top employer (large or small) is a company that provides a friendly atmosphere and is employee-focused. To others, a top employer is one that is perceived with better job security

---

21 Having successfully served its purpose the domain, **www.JobPlease.co.uk,** now redirects visitors to another website.

22 Kevin received quite a number of job leads since the ad was placed. Sadly, he died of cancer a few months later.

(i.e. a large company). Whatever you consider to be a top employer, here's three listings to get you started with your research *(page 61)*:

(1) The Sunday Times 100 best companies

business.timesonline.co.uk/tol/business/career_and_jobs/best_100_companies/best_100_tables

Alternative URL: **tinyurl.com/times-best100**

(2) All Companies listed on the London Stock Exchange [23]

www.londonstockexchange.com/statistics/companies-and-issuers/list-of-all-companies.xls

Alternative URL: **tinyurl.com/Stock-Exchange-List**

(3) Top employers list

See page 142.

Yellow Pages

Another great place to start any speculative job hunting is with your local Yellow Pages. If you don't have access to a copy it's probably just as well because the on-line version is far more useful for the job hunter anyway:

www.yell.com

Fig 18: Yellow Pages website

Once you're at the website, do a search for the company type (i.e. your industry) and try searching for companies in your local area. If nothing shows up then expand your search to your county etc. After you've short-listed a number of them then check to see if they have a website. If they do, see if they have a jobs page and bookmark it. Better still, try and register with the

23 This is a downloadable Excel Spreadsheet which can also be opened by OpenOffice.

website to get their job updates. If they don't have such a facility then monitor their jobs page *(see the section on "Web page changes" on page 88)*.

If they don't have a jobs page then you can send them a speculative job letter *(page 140)* anyway.

Self employment

If you've got expertise that companies need but cannot justify taking you on permanently then it might be worthwhile offering some consultancy work. The main drawback with this is that you'll be responsible for paying your own taxes. However, you could earn considerably more than you would if working for someone else.

By 'selling' your services you're not restricted to physical goods. In fact that is what you do when you work for someone else. You are selling your services to an employer.

For this you need to be well organised so think carefully before going down this route. Many books have been written on this subject so a trip to your local library will uncover some essential basics, including bookkeeping and marketing yourself. However, if nothing else, remember these four immortal words:

sell what people <u>want</u>

There is a sharp difference between what people **want** and what people need. People rarely buy what they need (unless they are forced to by law – things like car insurance springs to mind. People normally buy things emotionally and therefore spend their money on what they want (rather than using logic to buy what they need).

This may sound a bit obvious but many who set up a business for the first time totally miss this concept.

People often assume that the things they're interested in (like hobbies etc.), others must also be interested in also. Too many people have set up a shop in the High Street expecting people to flood to their doors only to be disappointed and close down soon after through lack of business.

So where can you get leads? They can come from your job hunting sources. Like I said, the same companies that employ people also take on people in a consultancy capacity (sometimes called contracts). Therefore don't exclude searching job sites for contract work as well as permanent vacancies.

Tips

If you're taking a career break to bring up a young family, you might be considering how you can get some extra income. How about becoming a Registered Childminder? You could get paid to look after other people's children while taking care of your own. The National Child Minding Association (NCMA) runs a number of courses in the UK and can offer you you some very useful advice. Their website is at:

www.ncma.org.uk

By the way, it's not just the mums who become childminders, many dads do too!

Tip 14: The National Child Minding Association

For more information and advice on self employment, visit the following websites:

Business Link

www.businesslink.gov.uk

Chambers of Commerce

www.britishchambers.org.uk

Citizens Advice Bureau

www.adviceguide.org.uk/index/life/employment/self-employment_checklist.htm

Alternative URL: **tinyurl.com/Citizens-Advice-Bureau**

Enterprise Agencies

England & Wales
www.nfea.com

Scotland
www.scottish-enterprise.com

HM Revenue and Customs

www.hmrc.gov.uk/businesses/tmastarting-up-in-business.shtml

Alternative URL: **tinyurl.com/HM-Revenue**

Small Business UK

www.smallbusiness.co.uk

This is Money

www.thisismoney.co.uk/smallbusiness

Your own bank

Visit your local branch and ask to speak to their Small Business Advisor.

Putting your job hunting on 'autopilot'

So far we've been searching the web, visiting on-line newspapers, job sites and individual company websites. We could do this day in and day out, over and over again. However, what if you could automate this process? That would certainly free up some of your time wouldn't it?

Well, there are four areas where you could get the power of the Internet to do some of the searching and send you the results by email. They are:

News alerts *(page 86)*

Web alerts *(page 87)*

Job alerts *(page 88)*

Web page changes *(page 88)*

News alerts

Keeping an eye on the latest news in your geographical area can uncover some great unadvertised jobs. For example, if a company is moving premises to your area or they have been awarded a large contract to fulfil; or have been offered a grant to expand their facilities then this is a good sign that they need extra staff. Early knowledge of this will create a distinct advantage and you should be quick to respond with a speculative job letter *(sample on page 115)*.

One of the quickest ways to find out (without frequently checking the news) is to set up a news alert. To do this, you can open up a free Google account (you also need an email account). If you haven't yet got an email account then check out the section on **setting up an email account** on page 26 right now.

To set up your automated alert, go to **Google Alerts**:

www.google.co.uk/alerts

After registering/logging on' you'll see the following options:

- **News**
- **Blogs**
- **Web**
- **Comprehensive**
- **Video**
- **Groups**

Choose the News Option and enter your search term, i.e. van driver (and set your alerts to daily):

"van driver" ~needed london

The '~'[24] in front of the word 'needed' means synonym. In this case, whenever the word 'needed' or anything with a similar meaning (i.e. wanted or required) is found in a news item (together with the phrase "van driver" and "London"), Google will send you an email with a link to the news article.

You should adjust the search term to suit your own particular job requirement. Sometimes a little experimentation is needed to get the best results.

Web alerts

This is very much the same as a news alert except that, if your search term appears anywhere on the web, Google will will send you an email with the links to relevant web pages. Your search term will vary slightly to a news item because you are specifically looking for a job posting. Your original search term should be sufficient:

"van driver" job london

24 If the ~ symbol is not displayed on your keyboard then hold down the 'Alt' key and type in 0126.

The 'comprehensive' option might seem to be the best choice because it enables you to receive notifications of News, Blogs, Web, Video, and Groups (Newsgroups). However, it will not make things easier for two reasons:

- Your search term will be slightly different for each medium. For example, you will rarely find jobs 'advertised' as news items so here you will be looking for clues as to whether there are possible job openings in your area.
- You will be spreading yourself too thinly and not focusing on the most likely sources of information for your geographical area. For example, it is unlikely that you will find many blogs specialising in jobs in your area or videos which might offer a clues as to where you can find work either.

To find out more about Google Alerts, take a look at their Help page at:

www.google.com/support/alerts

If you want to explore ways to improve your search results, go to the Google 'Cheat Sheet':

www.google.com/help/cheatsheet.html

Job alerts

Most good on-line job sites *(page 64)* have the ability to notify you of any new jobs by email. They are sometimes referred to as "Jobs by email" or "Job alerts" etc. An example is the Fish4Jobs website's job alerts:

www.fish4.co.uk/iad/myprofile/alerts

You will need to register with them before you can use the service.

Many of the top employers will also have the ability to email you when jobs are available. Many can be found on page 142.

Web page changes

There will be times when you want to monitor a specific web page with job listings. For example, you might be looking for a teaching job at a local college or university and frequently look at their appointments page. They may not be able to email you when specific jobs are available. In such cases you could use a free service like **Change Detection**. They will monitor any web page changes and automatically send you an email when there is an update.

To start monitoring web pages, go to:

www.changedetection.com

Job hunting is a numbers 'game'

Successful job hunting is very much like sales. If you talk to any professional sales person you'll realise that sales is a numbers 'game'. You won't make a sale to every customer you meet but you are sure to land some good ones if you keep at it.

> "A black belt = a white belt who never gave up!"
> *Sign on the wall of a martial arts centre.*

The more prospects you approach, the more sales you'll make. This is also true for job hunting. You will not have success with every application you send out. However, by sending out large numbers of them, you are sure to have some degree of success. Of course this also depends on the quality of the application.

Turning a refusal into a potential interview

Have you ever received a letter saying your application was unsuccessful? If not then you are either lucky or you just haven't applied for many jobs yet.

A common mistake made by job seekers is to take no action with refusal letters. There are a couple of things to bear in mind:

- The company was considerate, and cared enough to let you know the outcome. This means the company is still worth pursuing.
- Sometimes, a short-listed candidate may have had a change of heart – perhaps they've since accepted a job offer elsewhere; or they left a couple of weeks or so after starting the job.

Even at this stage you can salvage something out of the situation. On receiving a refusal letter you should write back to them saying that you were disappointed you were not short-listed for interview. You can also mention that, should the circumstances change or one of those short-listed candidates drop out, you would still be interested and pleased to be given the opportunity of an interview.

Believe it or not, this does work. Put yourself in the prospective employer's shoes. They've just sent out a lot of refusal letters and at least one of their candidates drops out. There wouldn't be enough time to contact all the unsuccessful candidates again. You, on the other hand have kept the door open and made it easy for them. You've shown initiative and confirmed your genuine interest in the company. Of course, they're going to re-consider you. Only if your CV really doesn't match their requirements would they not be interested in your offer.

See page 123 for a sample '**keep the door open**' letter you can send them. Make sure you mail it out on the same day as receiving their letter of refusal.

Becoming more employable

Even while job hunting, you must keep your skills updated and show a prospective employer that you are making the best use of your time whilst between jobs. They will undoubtedly forget that looking for a job can take up as much time as a full-time employment. However, rather that argue the point out with them at your interview, it would be wiser to make full use of your time.

What better use of any spare time than to undergo a course. There's plenty of opportunities around. You could contact your local jobcentre in the first instance and see if they have any job-related courses that would be useful. If not, you may wish to ask them about any grants available so you could take up a vocational course.

Visit your local college or university and see what courses they can offer too. Check out the following links:

Higher Education

www.ucas.ac.uk/students/coursesearch

Further Education

careersadvicefindacourse1.direct.gov.uk/pls/hot_ca/aff_page_pls_all_homepage?a=260405

Alternative URL: **tinyurl.com/UK-Courses**

Another option is to contact Learndirect to see what they can offer you. Their website is at:

www.learndirect.co.uk/browse/searchcourse

There are also a number of free on-line courses which could provide what you need. A listing of some of the more popular free courses, training & resources is shown at page 167.

If you're registered with Jobcentre Plus, you must check on any restrictions (i.e. number of study-hours per week) which may prevent you from receiving your full entitlement to financial benefits. They want to know that your course doesn't prevent you from getting a job.

Don't forget to be in touch with the appropriate professional body covering your job industry *(a list of the main ones are shown on page 155).* You will get some great help from these organisations. Many of them will also provide training.

Earlier on in your job hunting activities, you should have printed off some job specifications for the sort of jobs you are interested in. Have another look at these because they also suggest courses that would stand you in good stead for your next job interview *(page 62).*

Did you know that you may be eligible for an adult learning grant while studying? To find out more go to:

Direct Gov:
www.direct.gov.uk/en/EducationAndLearning/AdultLearning/FinancialHelpForAdultLearners/Adultlearninggrant/index.htm

Alternative URL: **tinyurl.com/Learning-Grant**

and

Learning Skills Council:

alg.lsc.gov.uk

Tips

For many supervisory and managerial jobs, good presentation skills are essential if you want to secure one of these positions. The following organisation provides excellent (and low cost) training which promotes both self confidence and good presentation skills:

Toastmasters International

www.toastmasters.org

Before you go off with the idea that this organisation is full of people in red jackets who do opening ceremonies etc. then think again! Nothing could be further from the truth.

To find a location near you click on the Find button on the left of their main web page:

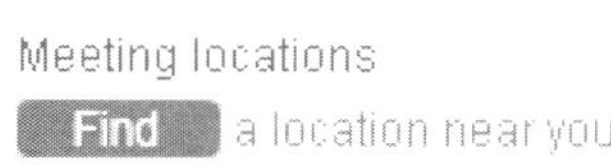

Check out their website and visit one of their locations near you. You'll be glad you did.

Tip 15: Toastmasters International

Your interviews

> "As you go to the interview, keep in mind that the person-who-has-the-power-to-hire-you is sweating, too. Why? Because, the hiring-interview is not a very reliable way to choose an employee."
> *Richard N. Bolles (1927 -), Author*[25].

So your CV was stunning and your cover letter caught the attention of the hiring manager. Your application has been moved to the top of the short-list and you have an interview – congratulations! You are now well on your way to getting the job.

Hold On! Just because you've got an interview, it doesn't mean your work is over. This is the time when you need to put in that extra effort to keep your name firmly in the mind of the hiring manager.

Hiring managers place their decision to employ people almost entirely on the interview. This is the make or break part of the job hunting process.

However, there is one lesser-known type of interview you should know about and that is the Telephone Interview.

The telephone interview

During your job hunt you could be invited to a telephone interview. This normally happens when:

- you applied for a job with a company that is a considerable distance away and they don't want you to travel all that way unless you have a good chance of being short-listed for the job.
- the job you applied for requires you to have good verbal communication skills.
- the prospective company have a large number of equally qualified candidates and need to short-list the best ones quickly.

25 Author of a best selling book called "What color is your parachute?"

These 'interviews' are really a way of screening candidates before the company selects the best one for the usual face-to-face interview. The screening usually lasts for about half an hour.

Normally you will be given sufficient notice before the interview date so you'll have time to get prepared. Ensure you have the following items close at hand:

- Your CV and covering letter[26]
- Portfolio
- Some notes or check-list of the most important points you want to make during the call.
- Ensure they call you on a land line rather than a mobile phone – you don't want the conversation to cut out because of poor reception

Preparing for a telephone interview isn't so much different to any other interview except that you do it from the comfort of your own home. However, this can be a problem because you don't want any family distractions while the interview is under way.

Treat this as the first interview and conduct your follow up action accordingly *(page 32)*.

Preparation for face-to-face interviews

Before attending the usual face-to-face interviews, it is equally important that you prepare for them in advance too. This preparation should start as soon as you've received notification of the interview.

Detailed research

It is absolutely vital that you conduct some research on the company before your interview. Your interviewer will ask questions to find out how well acquainted you are with them. Your response to these questions will demonstrate your true interest in the job and their company.

Before you begin, make sure you have a folder or binder handy to store your notes and print-outs relating to the company.

There are a number of on-line resources to help you get the most out of your research. The main ones are:

26 Be sure it is the same version that you sent to this company!

- **Companies House**
- **Company website**
- **Connexions Jobs 4 U database**
- **Corporate information**
- **Hemscott**
- **Kompass**

Companies House

If the company is incorporated[27], they will be registered with Companies House. Here, you can check the correct name and address of their Head Office:

www.companieshouse.gov.uk/toolsToHelp/findCompanyInfo.shtml

Alternative URL: **tinyurl.com/Company-House**

Tips

If you discover the head office of a registered company is at a solicitor's or accountancy firm then you may find that the company is small and the director works from home.

This is especially useful to know if you would rather work for a larger organisation where you can be part of a bigger team.

Being a very small company it could also mean that you may not get paid on time!

Tip 16: Identifying small companies

Company website

Check to see if the company have their own website. It should be advertised in any literature or letter headed paper. If not, go to Google and put in the search term (ensure you replace the following with the appropriate keywords):

[company name] [town/city]

27 i.e. Ltd or Plc.

For example, lets say we're looking for The Marriott International Hotel in London, we would feed the following information into the Google search engine:

marriott international london

If the company has a website it would show up in the search results. Visit the site and print off any pages of interest and place them in the folder you are preparing.

Connexions Jobs 4 U database

Although you won't find specific company information here, you will find lists of job families, articles and many job descriptions. It also includes links to other sources of information that will help you prepare for the interview.

You'll even find information here that isn't included on the company's website, literature, job description or person specification.

www.connexions-direct.com/jobs4u/index.cfm?pid=2

Alternative URL: **tinyurl.com/Jobs4U-Database**

Corporate Information

Information on global companies can be obtained from this website:

www.corporateinformation.com

For a fee you can obtain detailed financial information on many companies. However, you can also obtain a **free** snapshot on companies which still gives you enough background information to impress an interviewer.

For example, if we searched for 'Marriott Hotel' we could find this:

Hospitality Properties Trust Company Snapshot Purchase a Full Report on this Company

Business Description:

Hospitality Properties Trust. The Group's principal activity is invests in real estate used in hospitality industries. The Group operates in two segments namely hotel investments and travel center investments. Hotels are operated as Courtyard by Marriott, Candlewood Suites, Staybridge Suites, Residence Inn by Marriott, Crowne Plaza Hotels & Resorts, Hyatt PlaceTM, AmeriSuites, InterContinental Hotels & Resorts, Marriott Hotels and Resorts, Radisson Hotels & Resorts, TownePlace Suites by Marriott, Country Inns & Suites by Carlson, Holiday Inn Hotels & Resorts, Springhill Suites by Marriott, or Park Plaza Hotels & Resorts. As on 31-Dec-2008, the Group owned 289 hotels with 42,881 rooms or suites, and 185 travel centers. The Group operates in the United States, Canada and Puerto Rico.

Wright Quality Rating: **BCC2** Rating Explanations

Fig 19: Corporate information snapshot example

Hemscott

The following information can be obtained, from a number of large companies, by using the Hemscott website:

- Brief summary
- Turnover and pre-tax profit
- Key people
- Products brands and subsidiaries

Their website is at:

www.hemscott.com/companies/company-search.do

Alternative URL: **tinyurl.com/Hemscott**

Kompass

Kompass contains information on over 2 million companies, spanning more than 60 countries. The available information includes:

- products
- services
- address
- telephone/fax numbers
- website (if they have one)

The Kompass website can be found at:

www.kompass.com

Brush up on common interview questions

Another step in the preparation process is to go over some interview questions and have your answers already planned out. Most interviewers ask similar questions. This makes it easier for you to answer many of them. It will help you to remain confident throughout your interview.

A list of some of the more common questions are given on page 173.

Questions to ask the interviewer

Towards the end of the interview you will normally be invited to ask questions. Even if you're satisfied with the flow of the interview, you should still make a point of asking the interviewer some questions. Put together a list of them – about half a dozen should be sufficient. If you're stuck for something to ask, go to page 105 for some ideas.

Dry run

If the company isn't too far away, you could consider a dry run. Travelling to the company location, at the same time of day as the interview, will be useful if you've never been there before. This gives you an idea of what type of traffic you'll meet on the way. You will also feel more comfortable and at ease on the day of your interview by already knowing the lay of the land around the company.

The things to take into consideration are:

- **Choosing the right method of travel:**
  - **Bus**
  - **Car**
  - **Train**
- **Getting directions**
- **Weather forecast**
- **Punctuality**

Choosing the right method of travel

It sounds simple enough but it's surprising how many people leave this decision until the last moment. Not only that, they don't have any back up plan if things go wrong and end up being late for the interview.

Bus

Travelling by bus is by far the simplest way to travel. No need to worry about driving (let alone car parking problems). However, you don't want to be stuck on a bus for hours when a train will get you there much quicker.

To help you plan your journey, you can get your travel information from this website:

timetables.showbus.co.uk/busindex.htm

Car

In most cases, travelling by car will be the most convenient way to get to the interview. Before you travel, it would be wise to check for nearby parking facilities. On receiving your interview letter, contact the company to see if parking is available. If not, you should arrive at your destination in sufficient time to get to the nearest public car park.

Before the day of travel, check the car over to make sure that things like the fuel tank is full, battery is OK, radiator full, windscreen washers are full and working properly etc. Visit John Farlam's Smart Driving website for some useful info and check-lists:

Looking after your car

www.smartdriving.co.uk/Driving/You_and_your_car/index.htm

Alternative URL: **tinyurl.com/Smart-Drivers**

Perform the checks before the day of travel just in case you need to buy that extra screen wash or pump more air into the tyres. Leaving it until the last minute will create unnecessary stress and will have a negative impact on your interview. The last thing you need before your interview is for the car to break down!

Many people forget to check the likelihood of a traffic jam. Always allow extra time if the 'rush hour' coincides with your time of travel. The rush hours usually last from:

- **6 – 10 am (with a peak at around 8.30 am)**
- **12 Noon – 2pm (lunch-time traffic, with a peak around 1pm)**
- **4 – 7 pm (with a peak at around 5 pm)**

If you are lucky enough to avoid the rush hours then your travelling time will be considerably shorter.

Another consideration is roadworks and accidents which are a major cause of traffic jams. By tuning in to Radio 2 during busy periods you will get information on major areas of congestion.

Their frequency is:

- **FM: 88.1 MHz - 90.2 MHz**
- **DAB: 12B**

About an hour before departure, it would be wise to go online to the AA Roadwatch web site and enter the regions you will be travelling. Here you can discover anticipated congestion en route:

www.theaa.com/travelwatch/travel_news.jsp

Train

Travelling by train is less stressful than car. However, you should carefully choose your time of travel because trains do have a tendency to get cancelled every now and then. Because of this, catch an earlier one just in case.

For train enquiries, you can use the National Rail website:

www.nationalrail.co.uk

Don't forget to buy your tickets **before** the day of travel to avoid a queue at the ticket office!

Getting directions

It doesn't matter which method of travel you intend using, you'll need directions (unless you're familiar with the location of the interview). Google has a useful database of maps where you can even view the areas from detailed aerial photographs. Just enter the post code and zoom in!

Google Maps can be found at:

maps.google.co.uk

If you want directions, you can click on the "Get Directions" link below the Google Maps logo.

Weather forecast

On the day prior to travel, check out the weather forecast. If you are driving and the forecasted weather indicates excessive wind, rain, ice or snow then you'll need to allow extra travelling time. Local weather forecasts can be obtained from the BBC website at:

www.bbc.co.uk/weather

Even if you're using public transport, it would be nice to know if you need to take that umbrella, scarf and gloves with you!

Those little emergencies!

It doesn't matter how well you plan, some things do have a habit of going wrong. If you allow for little contingencies then you'll retain your composure for the interview. You might want to consider taking the following items with you (they don't take up that much space):

- **A couple of plasters**
- **Anti-antiperspirant** *(compact type)*
- **Breath freshener**
- **Comb**
- **Compact sewing kit** *(includes scissors, needle, thread and safety pins)*
- **Hand tissues**
- **Kiwi express sponge** *(or equivalent)*
- **Map and directions** *(including public car parks if travelling by car)*
- **Nail clippers**
- **Pen and notepad**
- **Tooth pick**
- **Transport timings**
- **Wet wipes (about half a dozen)**

The chances are that you probably won't need them. However, things like stepping into a muddy puddle, losing a button, sweating etc. can create the wrong impression. You wouldn't want to walk into any interview in those conditions!

Have your briefcase packed

For your interviews, you should have a suitable accessory for carrying your portfolio and other bulky items. A briefcase is the ideal answer. There are many types to choose from. Just make sure it's of a subtle colour that looks business-like. Black is the most commonly available colour.

Your briefcase should include the following:

- **'Emergency kit'**
- **Notebook** (A6 lined hard back is easily carried without looking too obtrusive – *page 10*)
- **Portfolio** *(page 40)*
- **Completed application form template** – NOT to be inserted in your portfolio but easily accessible *(page 53)*

- **Spare pens, pencils and eraser**
- **Three extra copies of your CV** (in addition to the one in your portfolio)
- **Form of identification such as your driving licence, passport, birth certificate** (or anything that was requested by the company in the letter of invitation you received from them[28])

The day before the interview

The biggest mistake that job seekers make is to leave some preparations until the day of travel. Here's a list of what you should have done before the interview day:

- **Brushed up on your answers to commonly asked interview questions** *(page 173)*
- **Decided on what to wear** *(page 102)*
- **Decided on your method of travel and made the necessary pre-travel arrangements** *(page 98)*
- **Memorised the questions to ask the interviewer** *(page 105)*
- **Packed your briefcase** *(page 101)*
- **Prepared your portfolio** *(page 40)*
- **Put together your 'emergency kit'** *(page 100)*
- **Researched the company** *(page 94)*

Attire

When attending interviews, dress appropriately for the occasion. There is a 'dress code' which is expected at most interviews and serves three purposes:

- People do 'choose books by their cover' and therefore a suit shows you in the best light. So you need to create a good first impression.
- Shows you are professional and have respect for the interviewers and company you want to work for.

---

28 Although these items are listed with the rest of the briefcase contents, you might consider carrying them in a more secure place to ensure their safekeeping.

- Gives a subliminal message to the interviewers which many of them unknowingly take into account when short-listing candidates.

There is an old saying:

> ***"You will never get a second chance to make a great first impression."***
> ***Origin Unknown.***

At the interview you should try to mirror the ethos of the company. You may be lucky enough to be told beforehand what to wear at the interview (i.e. if the interview includes practical exercises or selection tests which makes formal wear inappropriate). It's always better to over dress for an interview, if you're unsure of what is expected.

For a more casual interview, men could wear a button down shirt and tie with a good pair of trousers. Women could wear a nice blouse with dress slacks or a skirt.

The most important thing to remember when choosing an interview outfit is to make sure that you err on the conservative side. Tops should not be low cut and skirts should be no shorter then knee length for women.

For men, you'll want to keep the colour choices of your outfit on a more muted scale.

Ensure that your interview clothes fit well. If any don't, then it 'sends a message' to the interviewer that you don't plan ahead because you didn't even take the time to see that your clothes fitted properly. They will wonder if you lacked any planning skills needed for the job.

Your interview clothes should always be pressed and wrinkle free. Don't leave these preparations until the last minute. Your interview clothes need to be ready at a moment's notice. There may be times when you get a phone call asking you to attend an interview the very next day.

Hair should be neat and tidy and any make-up you wear needs to be subtle and understated. Refrain from using perfume or cologne on the day of the interview. If you need a subtle fragrance then use a good quality bath soap to wash with before leaving home. If you tend to perspire a lot then an odourless anti-antiperspirant may be necessary.

Accessories worn should not distract the interviewers' attention or they will be concentrating on what you are wearing rather than you.

If possible, have two or three interview outfits available. Apart from the fact that mishaps do happen, many jobs require more then one interview.

Therefore have a couple of outfits readily available for each interview that you go on.

If you don't have a decent outfit, and you are registered with Jobcentre Plus, you may want to ask for a discretionary grant to cover the cost of clothing to wear at an interview. Unless they no longer award such grants you will have no excuse for not looking your best for interviews.

If you are really short of cash, for a new suit, then you should consider visiting the local charity shops. You'll be amazed at some of the good quality suits available (albeit pre-owned). If it means the difference between getting a job or not then swallow your pride. You can always treat yourself to a new suit with your first or second pay packet!

What not-to-wear

It would seem obvious what you shouldn't wear at interviews. However, some candidates do turn up for interviews wearing the most inappropriate things. See page 176 for a list of the more common mistakes – make sure you are not caught out!

The day of the interview

So far you've been successful with your job application. You've done the preparations shown in the previous section (*"The day before the interview"*) on page 102).

You are now dressed and your briefcase is at the ready. Read the rest of this section to ensure you don't miss anything out.

Punctuality

After all the work you've put into the job hunt, you don't want to be late for the interview. Your interviewer might appear to empathise with you if your lateness is beyond your control. However, it will not create a very good impression. It's far better that the other candidates are late and you're the only one on time. Forward planning will ensure that you're not caught out.

Arrival

Aim to arrive at the interview venue about fifteen minutes early. This allows enough time to see the receptionist and walk through to meet the interviewers. Normally you'll wait at the reception and an interviewer will greet and escort you to where the interview will take place.

Despite all the preparations you've made you may still be asked to fill in another form while waiting. Bear this in mind because it also gives you an impression of the company itself. Maybe some of these forms should have been sent to you before the interview so that they could have been completed beforehand. If this is the case then the company may be a little disorganised and you probably won't want to work for them anyway.

If you haven't been sent an application form already, you might be given one at this point. Some companies use this as part of their selection process to see if you can recall facts, remain calm and write legibly. Be prepared for this by making sure you have a copy of your application form template tucked away in your briefcase *(see page 101)*. As long as it's kept up to date, transferring the information to another one will be a breeze and you'll retain your composure knowing the other candidates may not be so well prepared.

At the interview

When you meet the interviewer, maintain good eye contact, smile and give a firm handshake. You can tell quite a lot from a person's handshake. Follow the interviewer to the place you'll be having the interview but don't get over friendly at this point because it highlights your nervousness.

Take the seat the interviewer offers you. If you're wearing a coat, drape it over the back of the chair so that it doesn't get in the way.

Place your briefcase on the floor at your feet, and sit up straight with both feet on the floor. This will display good self-confidence.

Smile as you answer the questions and still maintain good eye contact without glaring. Experienced interviewers know that a lack of eye contact is a sign of a person who has something to hide or may not be completely honest. It is quite natural to be a nervous at an interview so don't make it seem as if you're not being truthful when answering questions.

Questions to ask the interviewer

Towards the end of the interview, you'll normally be given the opportunity to ask the interviewer some questions. Even if you're not, you should make a point of asking some anyway. This really shows that you do have an interest in both them and the company. If you can't come up with anything, try asking something like:

> **How does the company measure employee performance?**
>
> **What plans does the company have for the future?**
>
> **Can you tell me what part of the job you feel is the most challenging?**
>
> **When can I expect to be told the outcome of this interview?**

At the end of the interview, shake your interviewers' hand and thank them for their time.

Follow up

Following up after your interview is very important to ensure your name is at the forefront of the interviewer's mind throughout the hiring decision. They will be seeing a number of applicants over a period of time. Therefore a proper follow up is essential. It shows the interviewers that you really are interested in joining their company and it encourages them to favour you.

If you can demonstrate your ability to follow up on projects (i.e. the interview is really a mini project in itself) then don't you think they'll want someone like you joining their company? You will definitely have an advantage over the other candidates who assume that a decision has already been made at the interview itself.

There are two steps needed to ensure your name stays fresh in the interviewers mind:

- **Thank you letter**
- **Follow up call**

Thank you letter

Send a thank you letter, addressed to the main interviewer *(pages 32 and 33)*. Keep it short and to the point. Ideally, you should be sending the letter out on the same day as the interview.

Once the letter has been sent, enter the date into the progressive job log *(page 30)*.

The thank you letter should consist of three main paragraphs:

Paragraph 1

Thank the interviewer for taking the time to meet with you on the day of your interview. You need to mention the job that you discussed.

Paragraph 2

This gives you another chance to sell yourself for the job. Use key phrases from the job ad (or better still the job description/person specification) to highlight your strengths. This is a place to make the point that you're the right person for the job.

Paragraph 3

In your closing paragraph, thank the interviewer again for their time and consideration. Reiterate your interest and excitement about the position you applied for. Close your thank you letter by telling the interviewer that you look forward to hearing from them soon.

A sample interview thank you letter is shown on page 122.

Follow up call

The next follow up action is a telephone call *(pages 33 and 119).* Most interviewers will give you some idea when a decision will be made. If your interviewer did then use that time-line for planning a follow up call. If no indication was made then give two clear working days after the interview before making your your call.

Once the follow up call has been made, enter the date into the progressive job log *(page 30)* and tick the item off in your diary.

If you've received notification of the outcome then there's no need to make the follow up call.

As you wait for your job offer, continue with your job hunt and still attend all planned interviews you've arranged elsewhere. Never count on getting any job until you've received a written offer of employment.

Claiming back your travel costs

As long you're registered with Jobcentre Plus, you may well be eligible for a refund of travel costs. Speak to them as soon as you receive your interview letter. Take the letter with you, giving Jobcentre Plus plenty of time to arrange reimbursement or to issue you with a ticket for travel.

Conclusion

> "Finding a job is like fishing. You don't have to be a professional fisherman to catch fish. Anyone can catch fish: it just may take you a little longer."
> *Marvin Adams, Author.*[29]

Getting back to work quickly, even in a recession isn't an impossible task. However it does require patience and commitment on your part. To do this in the shortest time possible, you'll need to get yourself organised.

If you feel like giving up then talk to your friends and family (particularly those with a more positive outlook). If you speak to job seekers who say that it's a waste of time . . . or they dwell on the recession . . . etc. then ignore any advice they offer – **they're only going to drag you down to their level**.

Remember, these people are not job hunters but job seekers. The difference between you (the job hunter) and them is that you're a proactive 'get up and go person' (the very fact you're using this book indicates this). whereas they look for jobs, are unprepared, and don't follow through.

Remember to put in your best effort, be persistent, maintain your confidence and **you will succeed**.

Within your hands, you have one of the most powerful resources that's been put together for serious job hunters like you (this book)! So don't leave it on a bookshelf to gather dust – use it.

Believe it or not, there's only one overriding reason why hiring managers will select you rather than the other candidates for the job:

It's because they LIKE you!

Even hiring managers use their emotions to make what should be a logical decision *(although they won't admit it)*. If they sincerely like the look of you then this will influence their hiring decision (although it may be done at a subconscious level).

To your job hunting adventure (and ultimate success),

Brian P. Simms,
Get Me Off The Dole **www.GetMeOffTheDole.com**

29 Author of the book "Fast-track to your next job!: the complete no-nonsense guide", (2004).

Part III

Appendices

Appendices

Glossary

Abbr Used in this glossary to shorten the word Abbr..

A.S.A.P. Abbr. for as soon as possible.

ad Abbr. for advert; advertisement.

attire What you wear (i.e. for the interview).

avail Abbr. for available.

back up This is a fall back plan in case things go wrong. In computer terms, you would back up your CVs by making another copy of them and storing them away from the main file. If the main CV file failed to work then you would use your back up copy *(See Flash Drive).*

In job hunting, you would have a back up plan if your transport let you down, just to ensure you could still attend your interview for example.

Brainstorm Brainstorming is often used to generate new ideas. You would start with a central problem to solve and write down all possible solutions (included the far-fetched ones) as they come to you. It is better done in small groups. Once you have got your list together you then decide on the best solution. Sometimes the far-fetched solutions lead to better ones.

Chronolological Something that is in date order. In the case of CVs, the most recent item is shown first.

Browser A computer program that allows you to access websites on the Internet (World Wide Web).

c., approx Abbreviations for approximately.

co Abbr. for company.

comm Abbr. for communication.

cust Abbr. for customer.

Dialog Box When running programs, the computer will communicate with you by showing a screen prompt which recommends what to do next.

Dole A slang term used for unemployment. If someone is 'on the dole' then they are registered with Jobcentre Plus.

ess Abbr. for essential.

Ethos Refers to the culture and the way a company operates.

exc Abbr. for excellent.

exp Abbr. for experience.

f/t Abbr. for full time.

Flash Drive A small device, the size of a small penknife, which plugs into a computer to store back up copies of files.

Flyers Another term used for leaflets which are distributed by hand.

Gross As in gross pay. This is the amount of money you are paid before any deductions (i.e. tax etc.) are made *(see net)*.

gsm Abbr. for grams per square metre. It is a measure of the weight of paper. As a rule of thumb, the heavier the paper the better the print (however there are exceptions).

inc Abbr. for Inclusive – refers to salary.

Industry Sector A grouping of companies by the services or products they produce (i.e. Retail Sector).

Informational Interview A meeting in which a job hunter asks for advice rather than employment. It is a way of networking to obtain more job leads.

Inventory Normally refers to a list of physical items that is in stock. In this book it refers to your personal inventory– all of the skills etc. that you have about you.

job fair An event where several organisations and job hunters get together to discuss employment opportunities.

K Abbr. for thousand. Sometimes the salary would be expressed using this to save using three zeros, i.e. £25K.

Keyword A word (or phrase) used when searching for a website using search engines. It is sometimes referred to as search terms.

min Abbr. for minimum.

mth/mthly Abbr. for month/monthly.

Neg Abbr. for negotiable.

Net As is net pay. This is the amount of money you are left with after all deductions (i.e. tax etc.) are made *(see gross)*.

NI No Abbr for National Insurance number used for taxation purposes.

No. Abbr. for number.

Notepad A very basic form of word processing software that comes with Microsoft operating systems.

occ Abbr. for occasional.

p.w. Abbr. for Per week – refers to the amount of salary paid.

p/t Abbr. for part time.

pa Abbr. for Per Annum – Annual salary (not to be confused with PA meaning personal secretary).

Portfolio A collection of certificates, samples of work, details of experience etc. which you can show to an interviewer which gives an all-round picture of your capabilities *(page 40)*.

prep Abbr. for preparation.

prev Abbr. for previous.

pro rata According to the amount of time worked. In the case of part time working, your salary would be a percentage of the figure shown.

Ref No Abbr. for Reference number – particularly used in job ads where it refers to job reference numbers.

Referee A person who has agreed to write a reference for you on request from a prospective employer.

req Abbr. for required.

s.a.e. Abbr. for Stamped (or Self) Addressed Envelope.

Search terms See Keywords.

Sector See Industry Sector.

Speculative letter A speculative letter asks a prospective employer to consider you for vacancies within their company even though they may not have not advertised yet *(see Hidden job markets on page 70).*

SWOT Abbr. for Strengths, Weaknesses, Opportunities and Threats. Often used as a management evaluation tool (i.e. SWOT Analysis).

tba Abbr. for to be arranged.

trng, trg Abbr. for training.

URL Abbr. for Uniform Resource Locator (commonly known as the website address).

wk/wkly Abbr. for week/weekly.

Wordpad Another basic word-processing application by Microsoft. It is far more advanced than Notepad but it is not of a high standard for sustained business use. Microsoft Word is the standard used by businesses.

WP Abbr. For word-processing or word-processor.

Follow up call scripts

The following scripts are suggested outlines to get you started. You'll need to adjust them to suit your own situation:

- After a speculative letter has been sent
- After you responded to a job ad

Make sure you have your CV and any correspondence/information about the company (and the person you're calling) close to hand. You will also need your diary and notepaper.

After a speculative letter has been sent

(1) Call the person you sent your CV to. Smile as they pick up the phone and introduce yourself by saying something like:

" Good morning, [contacts name[30]]? Hi, my name is [your name]."

(2) Keep the momentum up and break the ice a little by saying something friendly such as:

"How are you today?"

(3) Wait for their comment and then get down to the real nature of your call by saying something along the lines of:

"[Contact's name], earlier this week [or last week whichever is appropriate] I sent you a letter with a copy of my CV. I just wanted to follow-up and see if you received it."

(4) If the other person says that they haven't received it etc. then say something like:

" I'm sorry to hear that you haven't received it yet."

(5) Keep the momentum up and continue with something like:

"I was really hoping to set up appointment to learn more about the career opportunity as a [job title you are interested in] in your company."

(6) This is where you are going to ask for the interview (but don't stop the flow of your conversation or give the other person a chance to say anything):

30 Say with a questioning tone to ensure that you are speaking to the right person.

"Are you able spare a few moments, later this week [or next week, depending on when you are calling them], to explore the opportunities with me?"

(7) The other person may say something to put you off. Whatever it is you should empathise with them (without being patronising) and be ready to 'think on your feet' a bit here:

"Oh, of course I do understand that [whatever their objection is]. A lot of good companies like [the company's name] [whatever is causing their objection].

This is precisely why I am calling you. I know how much you value your employees and always look for the best people".

(8) Continue with your flow and be ready to 'sell' yourself here (don't be overconfident with yourself and don't sound as if you're begging them either:

"I'd like to be amongst the first on your list when you begin to go through the CVs for that position. Can you take a few moments out of your busy schedule to meet so that we can discuss how my experience and skills could benefit your company?"

(9) If the other person still objects then don't push any more:

"I am sorry to hear that, although I do understand. However, would you please keep my details on file [or can I send you another CV to keep on file] should the situation change?"

(10)Follow through with the conversation and remain warm and polite. However, if they back down a little and agree to see you:

" Excellent. That's [confirm the date and time with them]. Thank you very much [contact's name]. I do appreciate you taking the time to speak with me – and for squeezing me into your busy schedule."

After you responded to a job advert

1st follow up call *(page 31)*

(1) Call the person who you sent your application to[31]. Smile as they pick up the phone and introduce yourself by saying something like:

31 Make sure you have your CV, covering letter and a copy of the job ad close at hand.

" Good morning, [contacts name[32]]? Hi, my name is [your name]."

(2) Keep the momentum up and break the ice a little by saying something friendly such as:

"How are you today?"

(3) Wait for their comment and then get down to the real nature of your call by saying something along the lines of:

"[Contact's name], last week [or whenever you sent your application] I wrote to you in response to your advert in [website or newspaper where you saw the advertisement] for a [job title applied for]. I just wanted to follow-up and see if you received it"

(4) If the other person says that they haven't received it etc. then say something like:

"I'm sorry to hear that you haven't received it yet. Can I email you a further copy or send one in the post?"

(5) It may well be that they lost your application or have already short-listed some candidates and you weren't amongst them.

Some companies don't bother to acknowledge applicants that aren't short-listed. In either case, they may be doing you a favour because they probably treat their own staff the same way. However, give them the benefit of the doubt and follow through with the conversation and send another CV by the fastest means.

(6) If they say that they have received your application then continue with something like:

"I'm glad to hear about that because I've heard that the mail is taking longer to get through these days."

(7) Keep the momentum by saying:

"I understand that the closing date is on [whatever the closing date is]. Can you give me an indication of when I may find out whether I have been short-listed?"

(8) The person you contacted will confirm the details.

(9) Afterwards, thank the contact and then make a note of this in your progressive job log *(page 30)* and your diary (as a first follow up call). Make sure you follow up about two working days after the date given.

---

32 Say with a questioning tone to ensure that you are speaking to the right person.

After the job application closing date

2nd follow up call *(page 32)*

(1) Call the person who you sent your application to[33]. Smile as they pick up the phone and introduce yourself by saying something like:

" Good morning, [contacts name[34]]? Hi, my name is [your name]."

(2) Keep the momentum up and break the ice a little by saying something friendly such as:

"How are you today?"

(3) Wait for their comment and then get down to the real nature of your call by saying something along the lines of:

"[Contact's name], last week [or whenever you sent your application] I wrote to you in response to your advert in [website or newspaper where you saw the advertisement] for a [job title applied for]. I just wanted to say that, because the mail seems to be taking longer to get through these days, I thought I would let you know that I haven't received any confirmation of Interview dates yet."

(4) If the other person says that they have received you application then skip to paragraph 10.

(5) If they say they haven't received your application then say something like:

"I contacted your company on [date you called them] and spoke to [mention the person you called – only if it isn't the person you are talking to now[35]] who said my application was received."

(6) Then go on to say "Does this mean that my application hasn't reached you yet?"

(7) Wait for their answer. It is likely that one of the following the following things happened:

- they mislaid your application
- your application was thrown out
- they haven't reached a decision yet

33 Make sure you have your CV, covering letter and a copy of the job ad close at hand.

34 Say with a questioning tone to ensure that you are speaking to the right person.

35 If the person you are speaking to confirmed receipt, you don't want to get into an argument with them – tread lightly here.

- the person who you are speaking to is not fully involved with the selection process

(8) Follow through with the conversation and remain calm, polite and keep smiling while you talk to them.

(9) It may well be that they mislaid your application or they have already short-listed some candidates and you weren't amongst them.

Some companies don't bother to acknowledge applicants that aren't short-listed. In either case, they may be doing you a favour because they probably treat their own staff the same way. However, give them the benefit of the doubt and follow through with the conversation and send another CV by the fastest means.

(10)If they say that they have received your application then continue with something like:

"I'm glad to hear about that because I have been a little concerned that your letter might have been delayed in the mail."

(11)Wait to hear what they have to say and respond accordingly. If they haven't made a decision yet then ask when you are likely to hear of the outcome (make a note of this in your diary for another follow up call if necessary).

After the 1st and 2nd interviews

3rd follow up call *(page 33)*

(1) Call the main person who interviewed you (there may be more than one of them)[36]. Smile as they pick up the phone and introduce yourself by saying something like:

" Good morning, [contacts name[37]]? Hi, my name is [your name]."

(2) Keep the momentum up and break the ice a little by saying something friendly such as:

"How are you today?"

(3) Wait for their comment and then get down to the real nature of your call by saying something along the lines of:

---

36 Make sure you have your CV, covering letter and a copy of the job ad close at hand.

37 Say with a questioning tone to ensure that you are speaking to the right person.

"[Contact's name], last week [or whenever you had your interview] We discussed the [job title] position and I would like to know if you have reached a decision."

(4) If they say no then ask:

"Is there anything else you'd like to know about my application that would help?"

(5) Wait to hear what they say and respond accordingly (making sure you have your CV and portfolio handy).

(6) Follow up by saying:

"I do understand that it must be quite a difficult decision. When can I expect to hear from you?"

(7) Listen to what they say and make a note in your diary and follow up again on a later date if necessary.

Progressive job log

4	3	2	1	Folio (Application No)
				Organisation/Company
				Contact
				Source
				CV Sent
				1st Follow Up Call
				2nd Follow Up Call
				1st Interview
				1st Thank You Letter
				3rd Follow Up Call
				2nd Interview
				2nd Thank You Letter
				4th Follow Up Call
				Outcome
				Comments

See Page 30 for details on completion

Fig 20: Progressive job log (enlarged)

Follow up letters

Job interview thank you letters *(pages 32 and 33)*

Soon after you get back from the interview, you must write a thank you letter to the interviewer. It's important to thank them for their time and consideration on the position that you were applying for. Ensure you mail the letter out by the very next morning.

Here's an example of an interview follow up letter. Change the wording to suit your own situation:

[Insert your address]

[Insert your contact telephone number]

[Insert hiring manager's name]
[Insert hiring manager's job title]
[Insert company/organisation address]

[Date]

Dear [Insert hiring manager's name]

[Job Title] ([Job Reference if any]) - Interview

I would like to thank you for giving me the opportunity to attend an interview [today or yesterday – whenever the interview took place] regarding the Retail Manager's position. I have learned even more from the interview and re-affirmed my desire to work for your company.

I am qualified and experienced to fulfil the duties required by the position. The [insert any new information about the company that you learned] was fascinating because I have experience [or replace with relevant qualifications] that would stand me in good stead for this position.

Should you need any further information regarding my career history then please do contact me.

Once again, many thanks for the time you spent with me at the interview, it was really appreciated.

I look forward to hearing from you soon.

Yours sincerely,

[Your full name]

Fig 21: Sample interview thank you letter

"Keep the door open" letter *(see page 32)*

Unfortunately, you'll receive letters of rejection. Don't take them personally because they have probably made a mistake by not short-listing you for the interview. You can turn this around and still keep the door open by giving the prospective employer another opportunity to contact you if any of their prime candidates don't measure up.

Here's an example of a door opener letter. Again, change the wording to suit your situation:

[Insert your address]

[Insert your contact telephone number]

[Insert hiring manager's name]
[Insert hiring manager's job title]
[Insert company/organisation address]

[Date]

Dear [Insert hiring manager's name]

[Job Title] ([Job Reference if any])

I was disappointed to hear that I wasn't short-listed for an interview in respect of the above post, although I do understand that a difficult decision was made.

However, I would like to let you know that I still am interested in working for your company and I do know that occasionally a candidate may not measure up to your expectations. Therefore, I will be only too pleased if you would contact me again should you have a change of heart.

In the meantime, if there is anything about my application that you would like to discuss further, then please do not hesitate to contact me. Should I not hear from you again, then I wish you every success in finding a suitable candidate for the position.

Yours sincerely,

[Your full name]

Fig 22: Sample "keep the door open" letter

Sample CVs

Chronological

[Your Full Name]
[Your address]
Tel: [telephone number] Fax: [fax number] Mob: [mobile phone number]
Email: [email address]

PERSONAL PROFILE

[Insert about three or four sentences/phrases here]

KEY SKILLS

[Insert about half a dozen key skills with bullet points]

CAREER/EMPLOYMENT HISTORY

[Insert dates of employment]	[Organisation], [Town or City] – [Job Title]
	[Briefly summarise your responsibilities, skills and any significant achievements]
[Insert dates of employment]	[Organisation], [Town or City] – [Job Title]
	[Briefly summarise your responsibilities, skills and any significant achievements]
[Insert dates of employment]	[Organisation], [Town or City] – [Job Title]
	[Briefly summarise your responsibilities, skills and any significant achievements]

PROFESSIONAL QUALIFICATIONS

[Insert brief details of any professional qualifications and memberships of professional bodies here if any. Otherwise ignore this section]

EDUCATION AND TRAINING

[Insert dates of study]	[Educational/Training organisation], [Town or City]
	[Briefly summarise the course titles and grades, qualifications, and any significant achievements]
[Insert dates of study]	[Educational/Training organisation], [Town or City]
	[Briefly summarise the course titles and grades,

	qualifications, and any significant achievements]
[Insert dates of study]	[Educational/Training organisation], [Town or City]
	[Briefly summarise the course titles and grades, qualifications, and any significant achievements]

INTERESTS

[Insert a brief summary of your hobbies, sports and interests]

Fig 23: Sample Chronological CV

Functional (or skills-led)

[Your Full Name]
[Your address]
Tel: [telephone number] Fax: [fax number] Mob: [mobile phone number]
Email: [email address]

PERSONAL PROFILE

[Insert about three or four sentences/phrases here]

[SKILL AREA]

[Bullet listing of what you have done in the past to show you are competent in this skills area]

[SKILL AREA]

[Bullet listing of what you can or have done in the past to show you are competent in this skills area]

[SKILL AREA]

[Bullet listing of what you can or have done in the past to show you are competent in this skills area]

EXPERIENCE

[Insert dates of employment]	**[Organisation], [Town or City] – [Job Title]**
[Insert dates of appointment]	[Job Title]
[Insert dates of appointment]	[Job Title]
[Insert dates of appointment]	[Job Title]
[Insert dates of employment]	**[Organisation], [Town or City] – [Job Title]**
[Insert dates of appointment]	[Job Title]
[Insert dates of appointment]	[Job Title]
[Insert dates of appointment]	[Job Title]
[Insert dates of employment]	**[Organisation], [Town or City] – [Job Title]**
[Insert dates of appointment]	[Job Title]
[Insert dates of appointment]	[Job Title]
[Insert dates of appointment]	[Job Title]

TRAINING

[Brief outline of all training undertaken – no dates necessary]

QUALIFICATIONS

[Listing of all professional and then educational/academic courses taken with their results/grates]

INTERESTS

[Insert a brief summary of your hobbies, sports and interests]

Fig 24: Sample Functional CV

Targeted (or combination)

[Your Full Name]
[Your address]
Tel: [telephone number] Fax: [fax number] Mob: [mobile phone number]
Email: [email address]

PERSONAL PROFILE

[Insert about three or four sentences/phrases here]

KEY SKILLS

[Insert about half a dozen key skills with bullet points]

CAREER & EDUCATION HISTORY

[INSERT DATE RANGE[38]]

[Job Title] – [Organisation], [Town or City]
[Job Title] – [Organisation], [Town or City]
[Job Title] – [Organisation], [Town or City]

Key Achievements

[Give brief details of your achievements across the jobs listed above to include anything quantifiable (i.e. financial or percentage increases/decreases) you were responsible for]

Key Skills Gained

[Give brief details of the skills you gained during this period which reflects the requirements of the job advert]

Professional Qualifications

[Insert brief details of any professional qualifications and memberships of professional bodies gained during this period. Otherwise ignore this section]

Education and Training

[Educational/Training organisation], [Town or City] – [Course Title] – [Result or Grade]

[Give a brief explanation on how the course helped you to gain any knowledge which is relevant to the skill requirements shown in the job advert]

[INSERT DATE RANGE[38]]

[Job Title] – [Organisation], [Town or City]
[Job Title] – [Organisation], [Town or City]
[Job Title] – [Organisation], [Town or City]

Key Achievements

[Give brief details of your achievements across the jobs listed above to include anything quantifiable (i.e. financial or percentage increases/decreases) you were responsible for]

Key Skills Gained

[Give brief details of the skills you gained during this period which reflects the requirements of the job advert]

Professional Qualifications

[Insert brief details of any professional qualifications and memberships of professional bodies gained during this period. Otherwise ignore this section]

Education and Training

[Educational/Training organisation], [Town or City] – [Course Title] – [Result or Grade]

[Give a brief explanation on how the course helped you to gain any knowledge which is relevant to the skill requirements shown in the job advert]

[INSERT DATE RANGE[38]]

[Job Title] – [Organisation], [Town or City]
[Job Title] – [Organisation], [Town or City]
[Job Title] – [Organisation], [Town or City]

Key Achievements

[Give brief details of your achievements across the jobs listed above to include anything quantifiable (i.e. financial or percentage increases/decreases) you were responsible for]

Key Skills Gained

[Give brief details of the skills you gained during this period which reflects the requirements of the job advert]

Professional Qualifications

[Insert brief details of any professional qualifications and memberships of professional bodies gained during this period. Otherwise ignore this section]

Education and Training

[Educational/Training organisation], [Town or City] – [Course Title] – [Result or Grade]

[Give a brief explanation on how the course helped you to gain any knowledge

38 Group the jobs where the roles are similar to each other and insert the overall date range.

which is relevant to the skill requirements shown in the job advert]

INTERESTS

[Insert a brief summary of your hobbies, sports and interests]

Fig 25: Sample Targeted (or Combination) CV

Sample Cover Letter

Here's an example of a cover letter. You must change the wording to suit your own situation:

[Insert your address]

[Insert your contact telephone number]

[Insert hiring manager's name[39]]
[Insert hiring manager's job title]
[Insert company/organisation address]

[Date]

Dear [Insert hiring manager's name]

Application for the post of Retail Manager (Job Ref: 1234)

I am writing in response to your advertisement about the Retail Manager's position, advertised in the Daily Echo of 15th January 2010.

I have six years experience as a shop floor manager, running a team of sales advisers for a leading electrical appliance retailer. During this period I have dramatically reduced the amount of time a customer queues at the checkouts during busy periods. This waiting time was cut by as much as 60%. It was achieved by reorganising the sales advisers' work schedules. The additional benefit to the store was that checkout staff were able to up sell more of our products which lead to an increase in sales of over 23%.

By training my team in other tasks around the store and sharing the workload accordingly, increased job satisfaction amongst the staff meant that absenteeism and sickness were also reduced. This greatly assisted busy periods when we saved on overtime payments.

I strongly believe that my experience, and achievements to date will prove to be an asset to your organisation, making me a strong candidate for this post. I would appreciate the opportunity of an interview where I can discuss the position further.

I enclose a copy of my CV.

Yours sincerely,

[Your full name]

Encl.[40]

Fig 26: Sample cover letter

39 The name should appear on the ad. If not, contact the company to find out (ensure you spell it correctly).

40 Ensure you enclose your CV with this letter.

Cover letter and CV power words

When polishing up your CV or writing the covering letter letter, you can use a selection of the following words. They will transform a dull and dreary document into something more dynamic and exciting for the prospective employer to read.

Tips

Instead of repeating any of the power words in your CV or covering letters, get hold of a thesaurus and find a synonym (an alternative word which means the same thing).

An excellent on-line thesaurus can be found at:

thesaurus.reference.com

Tip 17: Using a thesaurus with power words

Accelerated
Accomplished
Achieved
Acquired
Adapted
Addressed
Adjusted
Administered
Advertised
Advised
Allocated
Analysed
Answered
Appeared
Applied
Appointed
Appraised
Approved
Arbitrated
Arranged
Assembled
Assessed
Assigned
Assisted
Assumed
Assured
Attained
Audited
Augmented
Authored
Awarded
Bought
Briefed
Broadened
Brought
Budgeted
Built
Calculated
Captured
Catalogued
Categorised
Caused
Centralised
Chaired
Changed
Charted
Checked
Clarified
Classified
Closed
Coached
Collected
Combined
Commented
Communicated
Compared
Compiled
Completed
Composed
Computed
Conceived
Conceptualised
Concluded
Conducted

Considered
Consolidated
Constructed
Consulted
Contacted
Continued
Contracted
Controlled
Converted
Convinced
Coordinated
Copyrighted
Corrected
Corresponded
Counselled
Counted
Created
Critiqued
Cultivated
Cut
Dealt
Debugged
Decided
Decreased
Defined
Delegated
Delivered
Demonstrated
Described
Designated
Designed
Detected
Determined
Developed
Devised
Diagnosed
Directed
Discovered
Discussed
Dispatched
Distributed
Documented
Doubled
Drafted
Drove
Earned
Edited
Effected
Elicited
Eliminated
Empowered
Encouraged
Endorsed
Engineered
Enhanced
Enlarged
Enlisted
Ensured
Entered
Established
Estimated
Evaluated
Examined
Exceeded
Executed
Expanded
Expedited
Experienced
Experimented
Explained
Explored
Expressed
Extended
Facilitated
Filed
Filled
Financed
Fired
Flagged
Focused
Forecast
Formulated
Found
Founded
Gathered
Generated
Graded
Granted
Guided
Halved
Handled
Headed
Helped
Hired
Identified
Ignited
Implemented
Improved
Improvised
Incorporated
Increased
Indexed
Influenced
Initiated
Innovated
Inspected
Inspired
Installed
Instigated
Instituted
Instructed
Insured
Interpreted
Interviewed
Introduced
Invented
Inventoried
Invested
Investigated
Involved

Issued
Joined
Justified
Kept
Launched
Lead
Learned
Leased
Lectured
Led
Liaised
Licensed
Listed
Lobbied
Logged
Machined
Made
Maintained
Managed
Manufactured
Marketed
Matched
Measured
Mediated
Met
Modernised
Modified
Monitored
Motivated
Moved
Named
Navigated
Negated
Negotiated
Observed
Obtained
Opened
Operated
Ordered
Organised
Overhauled
Oversaw
Participated
Patented
Perceived
Performed
Persuaded
Placed
Planned
Posted
Prepared
Presented
Presided
Processed
Procured
Produced
Proficient
Programmed
Prohibited
Projected
Promoted
Proposed
Provided
Published
Purchased
Pursued
Qualified
Quantified
Questioned
Raised
Ranked
Rated
Realised
Received
Recognised
Recommended
Reconciled
Recorded
Recruited
Redesigned
Reduced
Referred
Registered
Regulated
Rehabilitated
Related
Reorganised
Repaired
Replaced
Replied
Reported
Represented
Rescued
Researched
Reserved
Resolved
Responded
Restored
Revamped
Reviewed
Revise
Revised
Saved
Scheduled
Screened
Selected
Served
Serviced
Set
Shaped
Shared
Showed
Simplified
Sold
Solved
Sorted
Sought
Sparked
Specified
Spoke

Staffed
Standardised
Started
Steered
Streamlined
Strengthened
Stressed
Stretched
Structured
Studied
Submitted
Substituted
Succeeded
Suggested
Summarised
Superseded
Supervised
Supplied
Supported
Surveyed
Systematised
Tackled
Targeted
Taught
Terminated
Tested
Took
Toured
Traced
Tracked
Traded
Trained
Transcribed
Transferred
Transformed
Translated
Transported
Travelled
Treated
Trimmed
Tripled
Turned
Tutored
Umpired
Uncovered
Understood
Understudied
Unified
Unravelled
Updated
Upgraded
Upsurged
Used
Utilised
Vended
Verbalised
Verified
Visited
Waged
Weighed
Widened
Won
Worked
Wrote

Personal profile phrases

The following is a list of phrases which can be copied or modified to suit your own situation. Do ensure that the phrases you use in your CV give an honest and positive impression of yourself. If in doubt, ask a friend or colleague to assist you.

Please note that some of the phrases contain "He [she]". Don't forget to delete the inappropriate one.

Tips

Use the Power words from page 132 to 'breathe' new life into the personal profile phrases in your CV. This will help make them unique to you. It's unlikely that many other job applicants will ever think of this!

In the opening sentence/phrase of your personal profile, replace the words "individual" or "person" with the job role you are looking for (i.e. Electrician, Personnel Manager, Sales Adviser etc.).

Tip 18: Combining power words with personal profile phrases

Phrases

A committed individual who displays a mature but friendly manner.

A compassionate and caring individual who develops an empathy with people when needed most.

A hard-working and highly committed individual who sees any task through until its satisfactory completion.

A hard working and practical-minded individual with a friendly nature.

A methodical person who has a keen eye for detail.

A most reliable and flexible person who displays effective interpersonal and communication skills

A most reliable individual with exemplary attendance and time-keeping.

A results-driven person who displays a logical and methodical approach to achieving his [her] objectives.

A self-driven and self-reliant individual who leads by example.

A self-motivated and enthusiastic individual who thrives on challenging situations.

A self-motivated and hard-working individual who has a hands-on approach to problem-solving.

A self-motivated and independent individual who is quick to learn new skills in an ever-changing environment.

A self-motivated individual who possesses excellent administrative and organisational skills.

A self-motivated person with excellent people skills, who can work on his [her] own or as an active team member.

A self-starter with excellent communication skills and a keen sense of humour.

A thoroughly reliable and dependable person who maintains high standards throughout.

A trustworthy and caring person with good communication skills,

A versatile and well-motivated person who has a strong will to succeed.

A versatile individual with an enquiring mind and an optimistic outlook.

A very capable person who can work unsupervised to meet strict deadlines.

A well organised individual who can prioritise workloads efficiently by using his [her] own initiative.

Ability to adapt to many situations and displays an empathy with most people.

Able to prioritise his [her] workload and keep to deadlines.

An enthusiastic and tolerant team player with good communication skills

An extremely reliable and dependable individual who consistently strives for quality.

An extremely versatile and capable person who manages budgets within stringent guidelines.

An honest, hard-working and reliable individual who takes great pride in ensuring that a job is done well.

An organised and adaptable person who has an innovative approach and is accustomed to working under tight deadlines.

Being a determined and decisive individual, he [she] uses uses his [her] initiative to develop innovative solutions to many problems.

Being a person of high integrity he [she] is reliable and dependable.

Being an excellent communicator he [she] has good leadership and interpersonal skills.

Being target-driven and proactive, he [she] works well under pressure and has the ability to meet tight deadlines when required.

Consistently maintains a methodical and rigorous approach to achieving tasks and objectives.

Creative, imaginative and enthusiastic, he [she] is a multi-skilled, individual who has a hands-on approach.

Displays great initiative, can generate innovative ideas and will follow through with them as required.

Enjoys being a productive team player although is quite happy to manage and steer the group in order to reach the desired objective.

Enjoys working in a challenging environment using his [her] own initiative to generate ideas and follow through with them.

Having a methodical approach to planning and organising he [she] is an exceptionally good time-manager.

Having excellent communication skills and a pleasant personality he [she] motivates others to exceed their targets.

Having good interpersonal skills, he [she] communicates well with people from all walks of life.

Having great initiative and communication skills, he [she] manages to prioritise tasks well.

He [she] communicates well both orally and in written work.

He [she] displays a great sense of humour even in the most difficult of situations

He [she] effectively prioritises workloads and pays close attention to minor detail.

He [she] is an effective team player who can work to deadlines whilst remaining composed and with a keen sense of humour.

He [she] is self-aware, always looking to grow and seeks new responsibilities irrespective of reward or recognition.

He [she] works well, whether as a team member or on his [her] own, to meet stringent deadlines whilst maintaining high standards.

Reliable and flexible with the ability to work on his [her] own initiative.

Thrives on challenging opportunities and persistently strives to surpass required targets.

Works well as an active team player and enjoys supporting others.

Sample speculative job letter

[Insert your address]

[Insert your contact telephone number]

[Insert contact1 name]
[Insert contact's job title]
[Insert company/organisation address]

[Date]

Dear [Insert contact name[41]]

I am currently seeking new career opportunities in [the area of your expertise] and would like to be considered for any suitable vacancies that you may have within your organisation.

My key skills are:

- [list your key skills here as bullet points]

I enclose a copy of my CV which I hope you will find of interest and should you require any further information please do not hesitate to contact me.

I look forward to hearing from you in the near future.

Yours sincerely,

[Your full name]

Encl.[42]

Fig 27: Sample speculative job letter

This is a very basic speculative letter. Try to include reasons why a prospective employer would want to see you. Have another look at the sample cover letter on page 131 to get some ideas.

41 Wherever possible, the contact name should be that of the hiring manager.

42 Ensure you enclose your CV.

Sample networking letter

[Insert your address]

[Insert your contact telephone number]

[Insert contact1 name]
[Insert contact's job title]
[Insert company/organisation address]

[Date]

Dear [Insert contact name]

I was referred to you by [name of your own network contact] from [company name] in [town or city]. He [or she] suggested that I get in touch with you because of your expertise in the [job sector you are interested in] industry.

My goal is to secure a [job type] position in [job sector]. I really would appreciate any advice you could offer me regarding career opportunities in the [job sector] industry, effective job search, and the best way to find job leads.

Any assistance you can offer me would be greatly appreciated. I look forward to getting in touch with you next week with a view to setting up a telephone informational interview[43].

Once again many thanks for your consideration.

Yours sincerely,

[your full name]

Fig 28: Sample networking letter

Remember, the purpose of this letter is not necessarily to get you a job interview with that person (although it could happen). You want them to take enough interest in you so you're recommend to their contacts. However, the main goal of this letter is to gain some tips (and possibly insider information) about how to improve your job prospects within the industry. It is particularly useful if you have very little work experience in that sector.

43 An Informational Interview is a meeting in which a job hunters ask for advice rather than employment (although it often leads to employment).

Top employers

The following is a list of the largest employers in the UK, listed in broad industry sectors. The non-governmental employers are amongst the top companies in the FTSE 500. These companies are more likely to ride the recession so if you are fortunate enough to be employed with any of them, your job should be relatively secure.

Please note that some of the web addresses (URLs) are not prefixed with "www" and some are a little long-winded so alternatives are given to assist you.

Aerospace & Defence

BAE Systems
www.baesystems.com/Careers

Cobham
www.cobham.com/careers.aspx

Armed Forces

Army
www.armyjobs.mod.uk

Royal Air Force
www.raf.mod.uk/careers

Royal Navy
www.royalnavy.mod.uk/server/show/nav.6022

Banking

Abbey National
www.jobsatabbey.com

Alliance & Leicester
www.alliance-leicester-careers.co.uk

Barclays
www.barclays.co.uk/careers

Bradford & Bingley
www.bbg.co.uk/bbg/careers

Britannia Building Society
www.britannia.co.uk/careers

Deutsche Bank
www.db.com/careers/en/index.html

HBOS
www.iwantextra.co.uk

HSBC
www.jobs.hsbc.co.uk

Lloyds TSB
www.lloydstsbjobs.com

Royal Bank of Scotland
www.rbs.com/careers01.asp

Beverages

Diageo
www.diageo-careers.com

Pernod Ricard
www.pernod-ricard.com/en/pages/157/pernod/Careers.html

Alternative URL: tinyurl.com/pernod

SAB Miller
www.sabmiller.com/index.asp?pageid=8

Scottish & Newcastle
www.scottish-newcastle.com/careers.aspx

Chemicals

British Vita
www.thevitagroup.com/Pages/locations_worldwide.aspx

Alternative URL: tinyurl.com/british-vita

Imperial Chemical Industries
www.akzonobel.com/careers/working_with_us

Johnson Matthey
www.matthey.com/careers

Construction & Materials

Aggregate Industries
www.aggregate.com/employment.aspx

BPB
www.bpb.com/main.asp?page=25

Carillion
www.carillionplc.com/careers

Delta
www.deltaplc.com/Our_Company/Employees/Careers

Lafarge
www.lafarge.co.uk/wps/portal

Laing (John)
www.laing.com/careers/index_careers.htm

Pilkington
www.pilkington.com/europe/uk+and+ireland/english/employment

Alternative URL: tinyurl.com/pilkington-glass

Watts Blake Bearne
www.wbbminerals.net/recruitment

Electricity

British Energy
www.british-energy.com/vacancies.php

Eon
www.eon-uk.com/Careers

International Power
www.ipplc.com/ipr/ourpeople

Scottish & Southern Energy
www.scottish-southern.co.uk/SSEInternet/PowerfulOpportunities/Public

Alternative URL: tinyurl.com/s-s-energy

Scottish Power
www.scottishpower.com/CareerOpportunities.htm

Electronic & Electrical Equipment

Invensys
www.invensys.com/contact_us/default.asp?
top_nav_id=11&nav_id=11

Alternative URL: tinyurl.com/invensys

The Laird Group
www.lairdtech.com/pages/jobPostings/careers.asp

Emergency Services

Fire Service
www.fireservice.co.uk/recruitment

National Health Service
www.nhscareers.nhs.uk

Police
www.allpolicejobs.co.uk

Financial Services

Express Service Europe
home3.express.com/uk/include/jobs_express.html

Alternative URL: tinyurl.com/-express-europe

Axa
jobs.axa.co.uk

Goldman Sachs
www2.goldmansachs.com/careers

KPMG
www.kpmg.co.uk/careers

Morgan Stanley UK
www.morganstanley.com/about/careers

Fixed line telecommunications

British Telecommunications
www.btplc.com/careercentre

Cable & Wireless
www.cw.com/careers

Food & Drug Retailers

Asda
www.asda.jobs

Boots Group
www.bootsjobs.com

Greggs
www.greggs.plc.uk/people/recruitment

Iceland
www.iceland.co.uk/careers

Morrisons
www.morrisons.co.uk/Corporate/Work-with-Morrisons

Safeway
www.safeway.com/Employment

Sainsburys
www.sainsburys.co.uk/aboutus/recruitment

Somerfield
www.somerfieldgroup.co.uk/index.asp?sid=5

Tesco
www.tesco-careers.com

Food Producers

Associated British Foods
abfoods.com/csr/employees.asp

Bakkavor (Geest)
www.bakkavor.com/about/working-for-us

Brake Bros
www.brakesgroup.co.uk/index.php?option=com_content&task=view&id=6&Itemid=3

Alternative URL: tinyurl.com/brake-bros

Cadbury Schweppes
www.cadbury.com/Careers

Express Dairies
www.milkdeliveries.co.uk/recruitment

Northern Foods
www.northern-foods.co.uk/careers.htm

Tate & Lyle
www.tateandlyle.com/TateAndLyle/careers

Unilever
www.unilever.co.uk/ourcompany/careers

Uniq
www.uniq.com/recruitment

Gas, Water & Multiutilities

Severn Trent
www.stwater.co.uk/server.php?show=nav.5626

Alternative URL: tinyurl.com/severn-trent

United Utilities
www.unitedutilities.com/Jobs.htm

General Industrials

Smiths
www.smiths-group.com/careers.aspx

Tomkins
www.tomkins.co.uk/tomk/careers

Health Care Equipment & Services

Smith & Nephew
global.smith-nephew.com/master/2491.htm

Industrial Engineering

Bodycote International
www.bodycote.com/?OB=7

Enodis
www.enodis.co.uk/?xhtml=xhtml/eno/uk/en/minisite/careers/default.html&xsl=minisite.xsl

Alternative URL: tinyurl.com/enodis

FKI
www.fki.co.uk/template.cfm?contentid=62

Industrial Metals & Mining

Corus
www.corusgroup.com/en/careers

Industrial Transportation

Salvesen (Christian)
www.salvesen.com/our-positions.0.76.0.0.gb.html

Life Insurance

Aviva
www.aviva.com/index.asp?pageid=8

Countrywide Assured
www.countrywiderecruitment.co.uk

Invesco
careers.invesco.co.uk/portal/site/ipcareers

Old Mutual
www.oldmutual.com/careers/index.jsp

Provident Financial
www.providentfinancial.com/plc/Careers.html

Media

BBC
jobs.bbc.co.uk

British Sky Broadcasting
jobs.sky.com

Daily Mail & General Trust
www.dmgtopportunities.com

EMAP
www.emap.com/employment.asp

EMI Group
www.emimusic.co.uk/vacancies_communications.html

ITV
www.itvjobs.com

Johnston Press
www.johnstonpress.co.uk/jpplc/careers

Taylor Nelson Sofres
www.tnsglobal.com/careers

Thomson Reuters
careers.thomsonreuters.com

Trinity Mirror
www.trinitymirror.com/careers

Virgin Media
careers.virginmedia.com

Mining

BHP Billiton
jobs.bhpbilliton.com

Lonmin
www.lonmin.com/careers.aspx?pageId=13

Rio Tinto
www.riotinto.com/index_careers.asp

Mobile Telecommunications

O2
www.o2careers.co.uk

Vodafone
careers.vodafone.co.uk

Oil & Gas Producers

BG Group
www.bg-group.com/CAREERS

BP
www.bp.com/careers

Oil Equipment & Services

AMEC
www.amec.com/careers.htm

Personal Goods

SSL International
www.ssl-international.com/Careers

Pharmaceuticals & Biotechnology

AstraZeneca
www.astrazeneca.co.uk/azcareers/index.asp

GlaxoSmithKline
www.gsk.com/careers

Nycomed Amersham
www.nycomed.com/en/Menu/Careers

General Retail

Arcadia
www.arcadiagroup.co.uk/careers

Body Shop International
www.thebodyshop.co.uk/page/jobs

Carphone Warehouse
www.careersatcarphone.com

Debenhams
www.debenhams-jobs.com

Dixons
www.dsgiplc.com/Layout.aspx?CatID=730d3985-ff44-42fa-ae03-a02bbfc2777e&ID=1ca30b71-24a0-4837-a6d8-538799632051

Alternative URL: tinyurl.com/dsgiplc

Great Universal Stores
www.homeretailgroup.com/home/careers

Inchcape
www.inchcape.com/careersatinchcape

Kingfisher
www.kingfisher.co.uk/index.asp?pageid=181

Marks & Spencer
corporate.marksandspencer.com/mscareers

Matalan
www.matalancareers.com

Mothercare
www.mothercarejobs.com

Next
careers.next.co.uk/Index.aspx

Smith (W H)
www.whsmithcareers.co.uk

Sytner Group
corporate.sytner.co.uk/careers

Software & Computer Services

CMG
www.capitalmanagementgroup.co.uk/recruitment.html

Computacenter
www.computacenter.com/careers

Logica
www.logica.co.uk/careers+with+us/5242

Misys
www.misys.com/html/careers

Support Services

Amey
www.amey.co.uk/Careers/tabid/59/Default.aspx

Atkins (W S)
www.atkinsglobal.com

Bunzl
www.bunzl.com/bunzl/careers/recruitment

Capita
www.capita.co.uk/careers

Civil Service
www.careers.civil-service.gov.uk

Davis Service
www.sunlight.co.uk/recruitment.htm

De La Rue
www.delarue.com/Display.aspx?&MasterId=a6b54c54-f7f5-4ed5-849d-25c17211e92f&NavigationId=677

Alternative URL: tinyurl.com/de-la-rue

Deloitte
www.deloitte.com/dtt/section_home/0,1041,sid%253D19618,00.html

Alternative URL: tinyurl.com/deloitte-careers

Ernst & Young
www.ey.com/global/content.nsf/international/Careers

Hays
www.hayscareers.com

Interserve
www.interserveplc.co.uk/plc/careers

Jarvis
www.jarvis-uk.com/jarvisplc/careers

Menzies (John)
www.johnmenziesplc.com/about-us/careers.php

Ministry of Defence (Civilian)
www.civilianjobs.mod.uk

MITIE
www.mitie.co.uk/Careers

Mott Macdonald
www.careers.mottmac.com

Mouchel
www.mouchel.com/careers

Premier Farnell
www.premierfarnell.com/premier_farnell/careers

PricewaterhouseCoopers
www.pwc.com/uk/eng/careers/main

RAC
www.rac.co.uk/web/careers

Royal Mail
www.royalmail.com/portal/rm/erecjump2?catId=500185&mediaId=16000165

Alternative URL: tinyurl.com/uk-royal-mail

Securicor
www.g4s.com/home/employment.htm

Serco
www.serco.com/careers

St Ives
www.st-ives.co.uk/careers/introduction.htm

Travis Perkins
www.tpcareers.co.uk

Wolseley
www.wolseleycareers.co.uk

Technology Hardware & Equipment

Marconi
www.rtp-marconi.com/careers/careers.htm

Spirent
www.spirent.com/about/index.cfm?WS=53&wt=1

Tobacco

British Tobacco
www.bat.com/group/sites/uk__3mnfen.nsf/vwPagesWebLive/DO52AFV2?opendocument&SKN=3

Alternative URL: tinyurl.com/ba-tobacco

Travel & Leisure

Arriva
www.arriva.co.uk/arriva/en/careers

Avis Europe
www.avis-europe.com/content-5

BAA
www.baa.com/portal/site/default/menuitem.3bd4901b1305f00498a5e186c02865a0

Alternative URL: tinyurl.com/baa-careers

Bourne Leisure
www.bournejobs.co.uk

British Airways
www.britishairwaysjobs.com

First Choice Holidays
www.firstchoice4jobs.co.uk

First Group
www.firstgroup.com/ukbus/careers

Go Ahead
www.go-ahead.com/Main.php?iCmsPageId=74

Greene King
www.greenekingjobs.co.uk

Hilton
www.careersathilton.com/uki

Marriott Hotels International
www.marriott.com/careers/CareerPaths.mi

Marstons
www.wdb.co.uk/Default.asp

Millennium & Copthorne Hotels
www.millenniumhotels.com/corporate/careers/careers.html

Alternative URL: tinyurl.com/millenium-hotels

Mitchells & Butlers
www.mbplc.com/index.asp?pageid=5

Alternative URL: tinyurl.com/mitchells-and-butler

National Express
www.nationalexpress.com/utilities/jobs.cfm

Network Rail
www.networkrail.co.uk/aspx/117.aspx

Pizza Express
www.pizzaexpresscareers.co.uk

Stagecoach
www.stagecoachbus.com/careers.html

Thomas Cook
www.thomascookvacancies.co.uk

Wetherspoon (J D)
www.jdwetherspoon.co.uk/jobs

Whitbread
www.whitbread.co.uk/index.cfm?id=careers

Other resources

Top companies supporting women's advancement
www.wherewomenwanttowork.com/women/default.asp

British professional organisations

If you are a member of any of the following organisations, you are strongly advised to stay in touch with them so you know what is going on in your sector. If you are not a member, then consider joining the one's most relevant to your career path (or at least, refer back to the particular professional body's website to find out about the latest developments or even job opportunities).

Keeping yourself up to speed with developments in your industry will be of great benefit to you when attending interviews. It'll give you additional confidence when answering any of those industry-related questions.

Association of Business Executives (ABE)
www.abeuk.com

Association of Chartered Certified Accountants (ACCA)
www.accaglobal.com

Association of Corporate Treasurers (ACT)
www.treasurers.org

Association of International Accountants (AIA)
www.aiaworldwide.com

Association of Public Analysts (APA)
www.publicanalyst.com

British Computer Society (BCS)
www.bcs.org

British Paramedic Association (BPA)
www.britishparamedic.org

British Psychological Society (BPS)
www.bps.org.uk

Cambridge Academy of Management (CAM)
www.cambridge-uk.org

Chartered Institute of Arbitrators (CIArb)
www.arbitrators.org

Chartered Institute of Architectural Technologists (CIAT)
www.ciat.org.uk

Chartered Institute of Bankers in Scotland (CIOBS)
www.ciobs.org.uk

Chartered Institute of Environmental Health (CIEH)
www.cieh.org

Chartered Institute of Housing (CIH)
www.cih.org

Chartered Institute of Journalists (CIoJ)
www.cioj.co.uk

Chartered Institute of Library and Information Professionals (CILIP)
www.cilip.org.uk

Chartered Institute of Linguists (IoL)
www.iol.org.uk

Chartered Institute of Logistics and Transport (CILT)
www.ciltuk.org.uk

Chartered Institute of Loss Adjusters (CILA)
www.cila.co.uk

Chartered Institute of Management Accountants (CIMA)
www.cimaglobal.com

Chartered Institute of Patent Attorneys (CIPA)
www.cipa.org.uk

Chartered Institute of Personnel and Development (CIPD)
www.cipd.co.uk

Chartered Institute of Public Finance and Accountancy (CIPFA)
www.cipfa.org.uk

Chartered Institute of Public Relations (CIPR)
www.cipr.co.uk

Chartered Institute of Purchasing and Supply (CIPS)
www.cips.org

Chartered Institute of Taxation (CIOT)
www.tax.org.uk

Chartered Institution of Water and Environmental Management (CIWEM)
www.ciwem.org

Chartered Insurance Institute (CII)
www.cii.co.uk

Chartered Management Institute (CMI)
www.managers.org.uk

Chartered Quality Institute (CQI)
www.thecqi.org

Chartered Society of Designers (CSD)
www.csd.org.uk

Chartered Society of Physiotherapy (CSP)
www.csp.org.uk

City & Guilds of London Institute (C&G)
www.cityandguilds.com

College of Teachers (COT)
www.collegeofteachers.ac.uk

Continuity Forum (BCM)
www.continuityforum.org

Energy Institute (EI)
www.energyinst.org.uk

Engineering Council UK (ECUK)
www.engc.org.uk

Faculty and Institute of Actuaries
www.actuaries.org.uk

Faculty of Advocates
www.advocates.org.uk

Freshwater Biological Association (FBA)
www.fba.org.uk

Geological Society of London
www.geolsoc.org.uk

iIFS School of Finance
www.ifslearning.ac.uk

Institute of Administrative Management (IAM)
www.instam.org

Institute of Biology (IOB)
www.iob.org

Institute of Chartered Accountants in England & Wales (ICAEW)
www1.icaew.co.uk

Institute of Chartered Accountants in Ireland (ICAI)
www.icai.ie

Institute of Chartered Accountants of Scotland (ICAS)
www.icas.org.uk

Institute of Chartered Foresters
www.charteredforesters.org

Institute of Chartered Secretaries and Administrators (ICSA)
www.icsa.org.uk

Institute of Chartered Shipbrokers (ICS)
www.ics.org.uk

Institute of Continuing Professional Development (InstCPD)
www.cpdinstitute.org

Institute of Directors (IOD)
www.iod.co.uk

Institute of Education (IOE)
www.ioe.ac.uk/

Institute for Archaeologists (IfA)
www.archaeologists.net

Institute of Internal Auditors, UK and Ireland (IIA UK)
www.iia.org.uk

Institute of Leadership & Management (ILM)
www.i-l-m.com

Institute of Legal Executives (ILEX)
www.ilex.org.uk

Institute of Management Specialists (IMS)
www.group-ims.com/management.htm

Institute of Manufacturing (IMANF)
www.group-ims.com/manufacturing.htm

Institute of Materials, Minerals and Mining (IOM)
www.iom3.org

Institute of Mathematics and its Applications (IMA)
www.ima.org.uk

Institute of Physics (IoP)
www.iop.org

Institute of Professional Financial Managers (IPFM)
www.ipfm.org

Institute of Tourist Guiding (ITG)
www.itg.org.uk

Institute of Transport Administration (IoTA)
www.iota.org.uk

Institution of Analysts and Programmers (IAP)
www.iap.org.uk

Institution of Chemical Engineers (IchemE)
www.icheme.org

Institution of Civil Engineers (ICE)
www.ice.org.uk

Institution of Engineering and Technology (IET)
www.theiet.org

Institution of Environmental Science (IES)
www.ies-uk.org.uk

Institution of Mechanical Engineers (ImechE)
www.imeche.org

Institution of Occupational Safety and Health (IOSH)
www.iosh.co.uk

Institution of Structural Engineers (IstructE)
www.istructe.org

International Professional Managers Association (IPMA)
www.ipma.co.uk

Law Society of Scotland
www.lawscot.org.uk

Linnean Society of London (LS)
www.linnean.org

National Childminding Association (NCMA)
www.ncma.org.uk

Northwest Photonics Association (NWPA)
www.nwphotonicsassociation.org.uk

Orthodontic Technicians Association (OTA)
www.orthota.co.uk

Palaeontological Association (PalAss)
www.palass.org

Professional Business and technical Management (PBTM)
www.group-ims.com/business.htm

Royal Academy of Engineering (RAEng)
www.raeng.org.uk

Royal Aeronautical Society (RaeS)
www.raes.org.uk

Royal Anthropological Institute (RAI)
www.therai.org.uk

Royal Asiatic Society
www.royalasiaticsociety.org

Royal Astronomical Society (RAS)
www.ras.org.uk

Royal College of Anaesthetists (RCOA)
www.rcoa.ac.uk

Royal College of General Practitioners (RCGP)
www.rcgp.org.uk

Royal College of Nursing (RCN)
www.rcn.org.uk

Royal College of Physicians and Surgeons of Glasgow (RCPSG)
www.rcpsg.ac.uk

Royal College of Physicians of Edinburgh (RCPE)
www.rcpe.ac.uk

Royal College of Physicians of London (RCP)
www.rcplondon.ac.uk

Royal College of Psychiatrists (RCPSYCH)
www.rcpsych.ac.uk

Royal College of Radiologists (RCR)
www.rcr.ac.uk

Royal College of Surgeons of Edinburgh (RCSED)
www.rcsed.ac.uk

Royal Economic Society (RES)
www.res.org.uk

Royal Geographical Society (RGS-IBG)
www.rgs.org

Royal Incorporation of Architects in Scotland (RIAS)
www.rias.org.uk

Royal Institute of British Architects (RIBA)
www.architecture.com

Royal Institute of Navigation (RIN)
www.rin.org.uk

Royal Society for Public Health (RSPH)
www.rsph.org.uk

Royal Institution of Chartered Surveyors (RICS)
www.rics.org

Royal Meteorological Society (RMetS)
www.rmets.org

Royal Pharmaceutical Society of Great Britain (RPSGB)
www.rpsgb.org.uk

Royal Society for Asian Affairs (RSAA)
www.rsaa.org.uk

Royal Society for the Promotion of Health (RSPH)
www.rsph.org

Royal Society for the encouragement of Arts (RSA)
www.thersa.org

Royal Society of Chemistry (RSC)
www.rsc.org

Royal Society of Medicine (RSM)
www.roysocmed.ac.uk

Royal Society of Ulster Architects (RSUA)
www.rsua.org.uk

Royal Statistical Society (RSS)
www.rss.org.uk

Royal Town Planning Institute (RTPI)
www.rtpi.org.uk

Society for the Environment (SocEnv)
www.socenv.org.uk

Society of Indexers (SI)
www.indexers.org.uk

Society of Operations Engineers (SOE)
www.soe.org.uk

The Academy of Executives and Administrators (AEA)
www.group-ims.com/executives.htm

The Academy of Multi-Skills (AMS)
www.group-ims.com/multiskills.htm

The Chartered Institute of Marketing (CIM)
www.cim.co.uk

The Institution of Railway Signal Engineers (IRSE)
www.irse.org

The Law Society (LS)
www.lawsociety.org.uk

The Micropalaeontological Society (TMS)
www.nhm.ac.uk/hosted_sites/tms

The Nautical Institute (NI)
www.nautinst.org

The Oxford Association of Management (OXIM)
www.oxim.org

The Property Consultants Society (PCS)
www.p-c-s.org.uk

The Records Management Society (RMS)
www.rms-gb.org.uk

The Society of Sales and Marketing (SSM)
www.ssm.org.uk

The Society of Trust and Estate Practitioners (STEP)
www.step.org

Women's Engineering Society (WES)
www.wes.org.uk

Popular trade magazines

OFF-LINE

Here you can browse through an extensive list of free Business, Computer, Engineering and Trade magazines, white papers, downloads and podcasts to find free resources which will help you to become an expert in your industry:

getmeoffthedole.tradepub.com

Simply complete the application form and submit it. All are absolutely free to professionals who qualify.

ON-LINE

This is by no means a definitive listing of all the on-line publications available but is a selection of some of the most popular ones.

Engineering

Stainless Steel Industry Magazine
Stainless steel technology, fabrication, and production.
www.ssind.mcmail.com

The Engineer On-line
Engineering technology news, features and recruitment.
www.theengineer.co.uk

Financial Planning

Financial Planning Interactive
News and editorials for financial planners and advisers.
www.financial-planning.com

Trade Finance
News and articles for importers and exporters, financiers and insurers.
www.tradefinancemagazine.com

Food Industry

The Caterer
Information about catering jobs, work in hotels, bars, restaurants and catering.
www.caterer.com

The Master's Table Magazine
Promotes the British food and restaurant scene.
www.masters-table.co.uk

Management

The Source
Journal for management in the public sector
www.thesourcepublishing.co.uk

Total Business Magazine
Articles in the technology, manufacturing and retail sectors.
www.totalbusiness.org.uk

Management Consultancy
Resources for the management consultancy trade.
www.managementconsultancy.co.uk

Manufacturing

Findlay Publications
Supplier databases, marketing services, and census information.
www.findlay.co.uk

Industrial Focus
Manufacturing news and resources for management and industry.
www.industrialfocus.co.uk

New Industrial Products
Product launches, services, and developments.
www.newindustrialproducts.co.uk

Mining

Bloomsbury Minerals Economics
Specialises in the worldwide copper market.
www.bloomsburyminerals.com

Industrial Minerals Information
Authority on non-metallic minerals
www.mineralnet.co.uk

Packaging

Dotpackaging
Resource of the worldwide packaging industry.
www.dotpackaging.com

Printing

Pre Press World
Pre-press and printing industry news and product information and directory of companies.
www.prepressworld.co.uk

Property

Estates Review
British journal of property development and management, including articles on energy efficiency.
www.estatesreview.com

Publishing

Publishing News
Book trade newspaper.
www.publishingnews.co.uk

The Book Seller
Publishers' magazine with news, job listings and membership services.
www.thebookseller.com

Telecommunications

Capacity Magazine

Telecommunications bandwidth and capacity trading magazine.
www.telcap.co.uk

Total Telecom

News for telecommunications professionals.
www.totaltele.com

Free courses, training & resources

UK sources

Alison

Digital Literacy & IT Skills, Enterprise & Business Skills, Financial & Economic Literacy, Health & Safety & Compliance, Health Literacy, Leadership & Management Training, Language Skills, Personal Development & Soft Skills and Teacher Training Courses.
alison.com

Beginners.co.uk

Over 650 tutorials relating to a wide variety of software applications.
tutorials.beginners.co.uk

BBC

BBC Guide to using a computer
www.bbc.co.uk/computertutor/computertutorone

Improve your English and Maths with Skillswise.
www.bbc.co.uk/skillswise

Learn to speak French, German, Spanish, Italian, Portugese, Greek or Chinese.
www.bbc.co.uk/languages

On-line Broadcast & New Media Courses.
www.bbctraining.com/onlineCourses.asp

On-line Learning Support and Advice
www.bbc.co.uk/learning/subjects/basic_skills.shtml

Webwise – learn how to use the Internet.
www.bbc.co.uk/webwise/course

Direct Gov

Learning for free (Advice)
www.direct.gov.uk/en/EducationAndLearning/AdultLearning/FinancialHelpForAdultLearners/DG_10033130

Alternative URL: **tinyurl.com/Learning-For-Free**

Email College

Business, Personal Development, Jobs & Careers, Health, Information Skills, Creativity & Ideas, Consumer Issues and Writing Guides Courses.
www.emailcollege.co.uk

Free computer Tutorials

All courses are aimed at complete beginners, so you don't need any experience to get started.
www.homeandlearn.co.uk

Help With PCs

Computer hardware & software courses and tutorials.
www.helpwithpcs.com/courses/Course.htm

Intute

Science, Engineering & Technology, Arts & Humanities, Social Sciences and Health & Life Sciences tutorials.
www.vts.intute.ac.uk

Learners.org.uk

Subject areas include ESOL, Games & Quizzes, Health & Hobbies, ICT, Literacy & Numeracy, Personal Development, Professional Development and Schools & Parenting.
www.learners.org.uk/show_title.html

Learning Space

Arts and History, Business and Management, Education, Health and Lifestyle, IT and Computing, Law, Mathematics and Statistics, Modern Languages, Science and Nature, Society, Study Skills and Technology course materials.
openlearn.open.ac.uk

NetSkills

Tonic – Learn how the internet works, finding & evaluating information on the web, Using on-line services & technologies and creating your own web site.
www.netskills.ac.uk/content/products/online/tonic.html

Skills 4 Success

They offer many business-related courses including some which are free including: Direct Marketing, Communicating for profit, Costing and Pricing, Customer Care, Management Accounting, Marketing, Reception Skills, Using IT in your business, Time Stress and management, Taxation, Personal Selling Skills, Managing Performance, Bookkeeping, Credit Control, Customer Care on the Telephone, Accounting With Computers, Advertising and Promotion, Effective Management, Employing People, Health and Safety, Negotiating Skills and Start your own Business.
www.skills-4-success.com/free_courses.asp

Vision2Learn

Computer skills, Job skills, Life skills and Sport skills Courses.
www.creatingcareers.net

USA sources

About.Com

Adobe Photoshop Basics Course
graphicssoft.about.com/c/ec/1.htm

Baycon Group

FREE Online Tutorials, ijncluding: Basic Word, Excel, PowerPoint, Access, Flash, Vista, XP, Windows 98, SQL and Paint Shop Pro.
www.baycongroup.com

Kutztown University of Pennsylvania

Over 80 on-demand programs including Accounting, Bilingual (English/Spanish), Business Operations and Management, Business Planning, Finance, Government, International Business, Legal, Management Development, Marketing, Sales, Small Business Tax, Starting & Growing a Business.
www.kutztownsbdc.org/course_listing.asp

Massachusetts Institute of Technology

Free lecture notes, exams, and videos from MIT. No registration required.
ocw.mit.edu/OcwWeb/web/about/about/index.htm

New York University

Free on-line textbooks, lecture notes, tutorials, and videos on Mathematics and Physics.
homepages.nyu.edu/~jmg336/index.html

Open learning Initiative (Carnegie Mellon)

Free on-line courses, including: Engineering Statics, Statistics, Causal and Statistical Reasoning, Modern Biology, Chemistry, Economics, French, Logic & Proofs, Physics, Empirical Research Methods, Computational Discrete Mathematics and Visual Communication Design.
oli.web.cmu.edu/openlearning/forstudents/freecourses/biology
Alternative URL: **tinyurl.com/Carnegie-Mellon**

Stanford University

Many academic courses are available for download for playing on iPods, PCs, and Macs. You may also burn them to CDs too.
itunes.stanford.edu

Tufts

Agriculture, Blender 3D Design, Health Sciences, Physics, Film Production, Environmental Issues and Zoology.
ocw.tufts.edu/CourseList

UC Irvine

Courses include Fundamentals of Business Analysis, Fundamentals of Personal Financial Planning, High School Courses, Medical Product Quality Systems, On-line Instructor Training, Physics 21: Science from Superheroes to Global Warming, Regulatory Requirements for Pharmaceutical Products, Spa Operations, Training & Human Resources Development and White Collar Crime.
ocw.uci.edu/courses

University of California, Berkeley

Biology, Chemistry, Cognitive Science, Computer Science, Economics, Education, Electrical Engineering, Engineering, English, Geography, History, Law Philosophy, Psychology, Public Health, Sociology and Statistics courses.
webcast.berkeley.edu/courses.php

University of Notre Dame

Offers a wide variety of academic courses including the sciences, foreign studies, politics, history, languages and philosophy.
ocw.nd.edu/courselist

Utah State University

Offers a wide variety of academic course materials covering most sciences.
ocw.usu.edu/courselist

Other sources

LANGMaster

Free on-line language courses in: English, German, French, Spanish and Italian.
www.langmaster.com/lmcom/com/web/en-gb/pages/free-language-online.aspx

University of Southern Queensland

Courses available in Object Oriented Programming in C++, Communication, Technology & Policy, Teaching Students with Special Needs: Behaviour Management, Technology & Society, Creating Interactive Multimedia, Exploring Teaching & Learning in Tertiary Contexts, Introduction to Tourism, and General Science.
ocw.usq.edu.au

Common interview questions

The following is a list of common interview questions you might encounter:

Tell me a little about yourself

This is not an open question to go into every little detail about your life. You need to keep your answer to this question very professional by giving a 1 to 2 minute summary of your professional life.

Describe a typical workday for you

This is where you will want to highlight the skills that you use in your current or most recent job that would be beneficial to the company. You want to make your day sound interesting, full of challenges and how you approached/solved those challenges.

Why are you leaving your job (or why did you leave your job)?

This can be a tricky question for many job hunters. If you are changing careers, you may want to highlight some of the reasons that you are changing industries.

The sort of answers that will work most of the time include that you are looking to work closer to home and that you are looking for a company that you can grow with.

Don't cover the topic of money, or bad-mouth your previous employer(s).

What is your best and what is your worse attribute?

Sometimes it is reworded by asking you what your strengths and weaknesses are.

Answering the first part of this question is often easy for most people in an interview. It is the second part that gives people trouble.

You need to say that something about you is bad, but you do not want the interviewer to see you in a bad light. You need to put a slight twist on the answer to make the weakness sound quite positive.

One possible answer to the worse attribute is that you are a perfectionist and that you tend to keep working on a project until you get every little detail right.

What interests you about the job?

This is where some of your research will come in handy. You can point out how some of the responsibilities that the employer listed in their job ad are the sort of things you are keen to work with and have some experience.

If appropriate, you can also point out that the company is at the cutting edge of your profession and that you want to grow with an industry leader.

Why would you like to work for us?

Consider this question carefully before answering. Mention the positive aspects of the job that you find attractive (leave out anything negative). Don't mention salary.

What is your salary expectation?

This is a tricky question to answer. On the one hand you don't want to undersell yourself and then again you don't want to appear greedy either. There are two answers you could give here:

If the question is asked toward the early part of the interview then say that it is difficult to say at this point without knowing more about the job itself and the responsibilities that will go with it.

You could ask them what the salary range is and then answer by saying that your experience would place you somewhere towards the top at the top end.

Are you considering any other positions at the moment?

As a job hunter, the answer is undoubtedly yes. However, don't tell them much and especially don't mention the names of the other companies either. Mention that you've have had offers.

What do you think of the last company you worked for?

This is a trick question to test if you are going to bad-mouth your last employer – don't do it. Remain positive about them.

Tell me what you know about our company

You should have done some research on the company beforehand and this is your chance to create a strong impression on the interviewer.

Now that you get the general idea on how to handle the questions, here's some more for you to work out an answer for yourself:

- Give me an overview of your skills and abilities?
- If one of your colleagues or friends were going to describe you, what do you thing they would say?
- Describe the sort of person you would find difficulty in working with?
- Do you prefer working alone?
- What you you understand by teamwork?
- Describe a particular time when you worked under pressure.
- How do you cope with interruptions?
- Have you ever trained others and if so, can you give details?
- What were your major achievements over the past year?
- Explain why do you feel you would be suited to this type of work.
- What do you do in your spare time?
- What are the sort of qualities you think will be needed for this job?

Interviews – what NOT to wear

The following is a list of the more common items which can ruin your chances of a successful interview. If anything is not included here then you should try to put yourself in the interviewer's position and ask yourself whether the item(s) you want to wear will have a negative impact on your chances of a successful interview. See page 102 for other advice.

Accessories

Carrying a rucksack

Headphones around your neck

Mobile phone switched on

Sunglasses

Trendy handbags

Body

Aftershaves/perfumes/colognes

Bare legs

Bright/heavy Make-up

Long/bright coloured fingernails

Showing cleavage

Unnatural hair colours or styles

Visible tattoos

Clothing

Belt doesn't match shoes

Fishnets or patterned stockings/tights

Ill-fitting clothes

Ill-matching socks

Jeans

Leather jackets

Out-of-date suits

Overbearing ties

Rumpled or stained clothing

Short skirts – not covering the thighs when seated

Short socks showing bare flesh when seated

Short-sleeved shirts

Shorts

Trousers worn too low or too tight

Visible underwear

Footwear

Boots

Open-toed/backless shoes

Scuffed/dirty footwear

Trainers

Jewellery

Earrings on men

Excessive Jewellery

Facial/Tongue jewellery

More than one pair of earrings on women

Freelance websites

The following is a list of freelance websites that offer the opportunity for people to bid/apply for contracts or projects. These are, by no means, the only freelance websites but just a selection of the more popular ones. Although a number of the projects are IT or Internet related there are many that do require other skills.

UK Based

Freelance:UK
www.freelanceuk.com

Freelancer
www.freelancer.co.uk

Freelancers Net
www.freelancers.net

Network Freelance
www.networkfreelance.co.uk

People 4 Business
www.people4business.com

People Per Hour
www.peopleperhour.com

International

All Freelance Directory
www.allfreelance.com

DoNanza
www.donanza.com

eLance
www.elance.com

Freelance Writing
www.freelancewriting.com

Get A Freelancer
www.getafreelancer.com

Guru
www.guru.com

iFreelance
www.ifreelance.com

List Bid
www.listbid.com

No Agencies Please
www.noagenciesplease.com

NUJ Freelance Directory
www.freelancedirectory.org/

PHP Freelancers
www.php-freelancers.com

Project 4 Hire
www.project4hire.com

Rent A Coder
www.rentacoder.com

Scriptlance
www.scriptlance.com

Further reading

ADAMS, M. (2004). *Fast-track to your next job!: the complete no-nonsense guide.* Lincoln, NE, IUniverse.

AL-JAJJOKA, S. (2004). *How to pass professional level psychometric tests.* London, Kogan Page.

ALEXANDER, J. (2005). *Find that job in ninety minutes: the quickest and most effective way to seek out and get that job you have always wanted.* The ninety minutes series. Cirencester, Management Books 2000.

ALEXANDER, L. (1996). *Surviving redundancy how to take charge of yourself and your future.* Plymouth, How To Books.

ALLEN, J. G. (2000). *The complete Q & A job interview book.* New York, John Wiley.

AMOS, J.-A. (2007). *Handling tough job interviews: be prepared, perform well, get the job.* Oxford, How To Books.

BARRETT, J. (2000). *Test yourself!: test your aptitude, personality and motivation and plan your career.* London, Kogan Page.

BISHOP-FIRTH, R. (2000). *The ultimate CV for managers & professionals: win senior managerial positions with an outstanding CV.* Oxford, How To Books.

BLOCK, J. A., & BETRUS, M. (1999). *101 best cover letters.* New York, McGraw-Hill.

BLOCK, J. A., & BETRUS, M. (1999). *101 more best resumes.* New York, McGraw-Hill.

BOLLES, R. N. (2008). *What color is your parachute?: a practical manual for job-hunters and career-changers.* Berkeley, Calif, Ten Speed.

BOOHER, D. D. (1997). *Get ahead! stay ahead!: learn the 70 most important career skills, traits, and attitudes to stay employed! get promoted! get a better job!* New York, McGraw-Hill.

GERBERG, R. J. (2003). *The McKenzie Scott executive job search system: our client handbook, part I.* Denver, CO, McKenzie Scott Press.

EGGERT, M. (2007). *Perfect CV.* London, Random House.

HIRSH, W. (2003). *Six weeks to find a job.* London, Hodder & Stoughton.

HODGSON, S. (2008). *A-Z of careers & jobs.* London, Kogan Page.

JACKSON, T., & JACKSON, E. (1996). *The perfect CV: how to get the job you really want.* London, Piatkus.

JOHNSTONE, J. (2004). *The job application handbook: how to sell yourself to an employer using proven strategies and effective techniques.* Oxford, How To Books.

KENT, S. (2002). *Odd jobs: unusual ways to earn a living.* London, Kogan Page.

KRECHOWIECKA, I. (2002). *The Times A-Z of careers & jobs.* London, Kogan Page.

MCGEE, P. (1997). *Writing a CV that works how to develop and use your key marketing tool.* Oxford, How to Books.

SATTERTHWAITE, F., & D'ORSI, G. (2003). *The career portfolio workbook using the newest tool in your job-hunting arsenal to impress employers and land a great job.* New York, McGraw-Hill.

WEBB, R. (1997). *Making applications.* Graduate careers information. Manchester, Careers Services Trust.

WEEKS, W. (1996). *How to get the top jobs that are never advertised.* London, Kogan Page.

WEINSTEIN, B. (1996). *Who says there are no jobs out there?: 25 irreverent rules for getting a job.* London, McGraw-Hill.

WHITMORE, T. (2009). *How to write an impressive CV and cover letter : a comprehensive guide for the UK job seeker.* Begbroke, Oxford, United Kingdon, How To Books, Ltd.

WILLIAMS, L. (1996). *Readymade CVs: a source book for job hunters.* London, Kogan Page.

WILLIAMS, L. (2000). *Readymade job search letters: every type of letter for getting the job you want.* London, Kogan Page.

YEUNG, R. (2007). *Job-hunting and career-change all-in-one for dummies.* Chichester, Wiley.

Index

Index

1108321R0

Printed in Great Britain by
Amazon.co.uk, Ltd.,
Marston Gate.